Essential Series

Springer

London
Berlin
Heidelberg
New York
Barcelona
Hong Kong
Milan
Paris
Singapore
Tokyo

Fiaz Hussain

Essential
Flash 5.0
fast

Rapid Web Animation

Springer

Fiaz Hussain BSc (Hons), MSc, PhD
Dubai Polytechnic, PO Box 1457, Dubai, United Arab Emirates

Series Editor
John Cowell, BSc (Hons), MPhil, PhD
Department of Computer Science, De Montfort University, The Gateway,
Leicester LE1 9BH

British Library Cataloguing in Publication Data
Hussain, Fiaz
  Essential Flash 5.0 fast : rapid Web animation. –
  (Essential series)
  1. Macromedia Flash (Computer file)
  I. Title II. Flash 5.0 fast
  006.7'869
ISBN 1852334517

Library of Congress Cataloging-in-Publication Data
Hussain, Fiaz, 1960-
    Essential Flash 5.0 fast : Rapid Web Animation / Fiaz Hussain.
       p. cm. – (Essential series)
    ISBN 1-85233-451-7 (alk. paper)
      1. Computer animation. 2. Flash (computer file) 3. Web sites—Authoring programs. I.
    Title. II. Essential series (Springer-Verlag)
TR897.7 .H87 2001
006.6'96—dc21
                                                                        2001031425

ISBN 1-85233-451-7 Springer-Verlag London Berlin Heidelberg
a member of BertelsmannSpringer Science+Business Media GmbH
http://www.springer.co.uk

Typesetting: Mac Style, Scarborough, N. Yorkshire
Printed and bound at The Cromwell Press, Trowbridge, Wiltshire
34/3830-543210 Printed on acid-free paper SPIN 10793540

Dedication

To all the pioneers, whose commitment and perspiration led
to a moment of inspiration benefiting the global community.

Acknowledgements

I am grateful to Dr John Cowell, De Montfort University, for his encouragement and his super support throughout the development of this manuscript. I am also grateful to Professor John Vince, Bournemouth University, for making helpful suggestions and providing motivation for the project. The team at Springer has provided a lot of assistance. I would, in particular, like to thank Beverley Ford and Rebecca Mowat for their endurance and guidance. Finally, and by no means least, a special thank you to my family: to my wife, Shabana, and my two children, Luqman and Batool. If it wasn't for their understanding, patience and affection, it would have been impossible to write a single word, yet alone a complete book.

Preface

The development of the Internet has provided opportunities to a whole host of communities across the globe to communicate and to learn together. People with different culture, heritage and language are able to convey messages and interact like never before. In fact, only a decade ago such communication was limited to scientists or professionals working on a particular project to share ideas using electronic mail (e-mail). Today, there are millions of people using the Internet for entertainment and business purposes. Moreover, there are countless web-sites enticing individuals to browse and buy. With so much choice for the user, it is paramount that web-sites are not just attractive, but also do not take too long to download true colour images and animations. The longer the user waits, the more chance they will move on to another site.

Macromedia's Flash is an ideal platform for designers and web developers since it provides a comprehensive authoring environment and a multitude of publishing options. Working with vectors, instead of bitmaps, it aims at providing high quality animations, but with a resulting file size that can be quickly downloaded. It works with all the well-known formats, including GIF, animated GIF, JPEG, PNG, QuickTime and HTML. Each format has parameters which can be used to customize the final Flash movie.

Flash 5.0 builds on the popular previous version of Flash 4.0. It includes improved artwork features (fill, stroke, colour, etc.) which are now available through a set of panels. The panels can be made to float on the screen and thus allowing easy access to the numerous sets of options. There are panels for working with strokes, fills, colour, text, frames, instances and actions. There is also a new tool, the Pen tool, that allows for defining paths and having better control, for example, on the shape of an object. Interactivity can be added via the relevant panel settings or can be written using Macromedia's ActionScript. This is a scripting language which allows for greater control of the final Flash movie. Other attractions include the Movie Explorer which displays the contents of the entire movie, Print actions that can be used to control printable frames and support for importing MP3 sound files.

Essential Flash 5.0 has been written to provide an easy, but informative, introduction to the world of Flash. It begins with introducing the development environment and ends with showing how to publish the final movie. It is primarily aimed at readers who may be new to Flash 5.0 and who are looking for a quick start to getting a web-site published using the sophisticated tools and features available. The book is also structured, with eleven chapters, to provide a basis for introducing the Flash 5.0 environment in the classroom. The style of writing is deliberately preparative to allow for the maximum absorption and learning of Flash 5.0 to take place, in the shortest possible time.

Finally, it should be noted that Macromedia provides comprehensive support for its products, including Flash 5.0. This includes copies of manuals and links to discussion forums. The Macromedia web-site is located at www.macromedia.com.

Writing a book of such a size can always be improved. I would therefore welcome any comments and suggestions, together with notification of any omissions. My email address is fiaz@computer.org and I look forward to hearing from you. I wish you every success using Flash 5.0.

Fiaz Hussain
January 2001

Contents

Contents

Flash Environment

Introduction

Macromedia Flash 5.0 provides an exciting environment to design and create interactive animation suitable primarily for web publishing. The comprehensive range of features available can, initially, seem overwhelming. Indeed, the type of sophistication embedded in some of the features takes time to absorb, though once learnt the real power of Flash can be used to create attractive and dynamic pages at relative ease. As we will see, the development of such pages can be achieved by using merely the graphical interface or through inserting added control by using, for example, scripts.

In this chapter, we take an introductory journey to understanding some of the components making up the environment. In this regard, we will look at:

- the stage
- the toolbars
- the timeline
- the panels.

The environment

Having installed and run Flash, the user typically gets a screen similar to that shown in Figure 1.1. The interface consists of several components, some of which are identified in the figure. The Stage is the space used to create a Flash movie. Through using the Toolbox (discussed later in this chapter), attractive graphics such as logos can be produced. If we are looking at creating any kind of animation then the Timeline comes into play. There is also a set of Panels which assist in viewing and editing properties relating to objects, frames, scenes, etc. We will start with understanding the Stage, Toolbox and then the Timeline. In doing so, we will learn about some of the options that are available to us to customize the environment so that it meets our intended production. We will then briefly look at Panels (further details of which can be found in the relevant chapters).

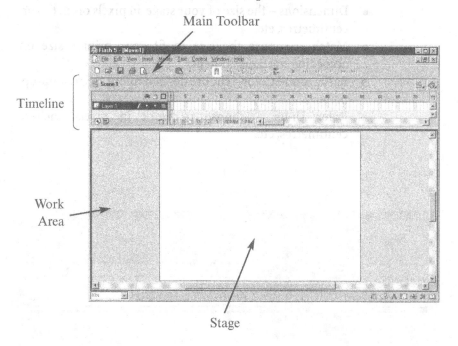

Figure 1.1 The Flash interface.

The Stage

Flash movies consist of a series of frames, each frame depicting a change of scene. At any one moment of time, the Stage shows the composition of a frame. In other words, the Stage is used to create the contents of a single frame. Associated with the Stage is a corresponding dialogue box. This is referred to as the Movie Properties dialogue box. The can be activated through either the Modify menu, or via the frame rate option available on the Timeline, or CTRL+M. The former two selection options are shown in Figures 1.2 and 1.3, respectively.

The Movie Properties dialogue box is shown in Figure 1.4. The parameters associated with this and, therefore, those that determine the settings for the Stage are as follows:

- Frame Rate – the number of frames per second (more on this later)
- Dimensions – the size of your stage, in pixels or inches or centimetres, etc.
- Match – choose the size to fit your printer size or according to frame contents
- Background Color – choose desired colour from a pop-up menu
- Ruler Units – choose to work in pixels, inches, centimetres, etc.

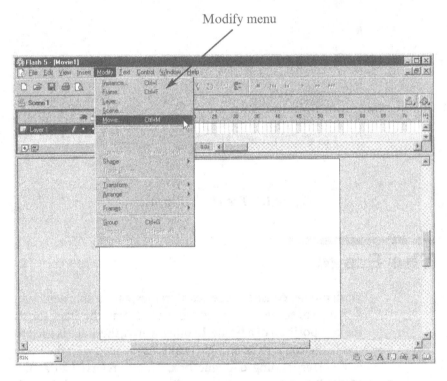

Figure 1.2 *Selecting the Movies Properties dialogue box via the* `Modify | Movie` *option.*

It is possible to convert between units or to work with one type (for example, inches) and then change this to another type (say, pixels). The option Ruler Units can be used for this. In this case, if we wanted our picture to be 4 inches wide and

2 inches high, then we would start with a setting of inches and type in 4 and 2 respectively in the Dimensions boxes. Having done this, we can convert to pixels by simply changing the Ruler Units from Inches to Pixels. The width and height should now read 288 px and 144 px respectively. You may want to verify that this is the case. There is also a predefined resolution (that is, dimensions) for the Stage. This is shown in Table 1.1.

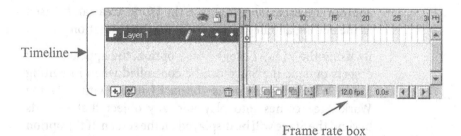

Timeline →

Frame rate box

***Figure 1.3** Selecting the Movie Properties dialogue box through (double-clicking) the frame rate box on the Timeline, as shown.*

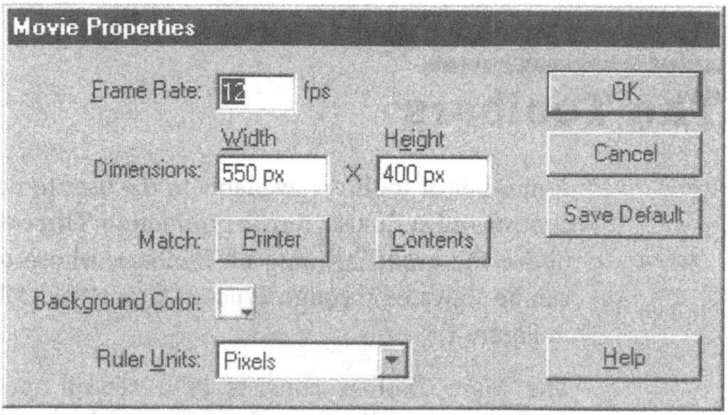

***Figure 1.4** The Movie Properties dialogue box, used to customize settings for the Stage.*

Having customized the parameters for the Stage, the Save Default button (see Figure 1.4) allows you to store these for all new productions.

In Figure 1.1, we also note that the environment includes a Work Area which lies outside the Stage. As the name suggests, any objects appearing in this area are seen not to be part of a Flash movie. This includes objects which are partially on the Stage and partially outside. Whatever portion is on the Stage will be visible in a Flash movie, whilst objects or its sections lying within the Work Area will not be. This allows the user to develop a design and to include it in a movie on an appropriate occasion. Moreover, the Work Area can be used as the ending and beginning point for the animation.

By using the View | Work Area option, the appearance of objects outside the Stage can be controlled when in editing mode. When this option is checked (shown with a ü), the Work Area comes into play and any object that extends beyond the Stage will be displayed on the screen. If the option is not checked then only what is on the Stage is displayed.

Table 1.1 Size resolutions for the Stage.

Dimensions	Inches	Centimetres	Pixels
Minimum: Width x Height	0.25 x 0.25	0.63 x 0.63	18 x 18
Maximum: Width x Height	40 x 40	101.05 x 101.05	2880 x 2880

The Toolbars

A number of tools are available to the user to design, create, control and evaluate a movie production. Three of these come under the broad heading of Toolbars, whose dialogue box can be activated through Window | Toolbars. This is shown in Figure 1.5.

The Main Toolbar consists of a set of options for file management, editing, and some useful creativity buttons. These are shown in Figure 1.6. We will be looking at the creativity buttons a little later.

The Status Toolbar (line) provides information relevant at the time of application. For example, when choosing to select a feature, some details about this are displayed. In addition to this, the Status Toolbar contains entries for the Caps Lock and Num Lock keys.

The Controller Toolbar has the well-known VCR buttons for play, stop, step rewind, step forward, rewind to start and fast forward to end. Figure 1.7 illustrates the set-up. This toolbar comes into play mainly when there is a need to evaluate a movie (for example, to test to see how the animation will look).

In addition to these three toolbars, Flash 5.0 also has a Launcher Bar and a ToolBox. As Figure 1.8 shows, the Launcher bar contains the zoom control menu, as well as the panel selection options. It is located at the bottom of the application (Stage) window. The zoom control menu contains (in addition to the usual percentage zoom values) two options: Show Frame and Show All. The former adjusts the magnification for the Stage so that it covers the display window. The Show All option magnifies with reference to the objects on the Stage. In other words, the area occupied by the objects is adjusted (normally increased to cover the display window). On the Launcher Bar, there are seven panels, namely info, mixer, character, instance, movie explorer, actions, and library. These launch (show and hide) dialogue cards representing the respective feature. Some of these panels are discussed briefly in the latter part of this chapter, though most of the description is left to the other chapters dealing with the respective topics.

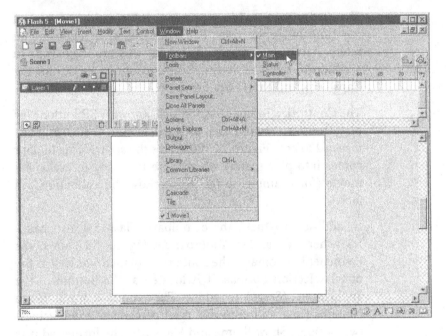

Figure 1.5 *Selection of three Toolbars: Main, Status and Controller.*

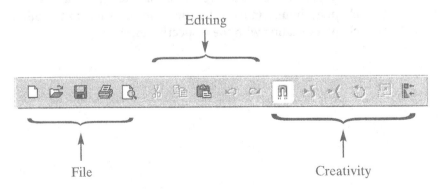

Figure 1.6 *The Main Toolbar.*

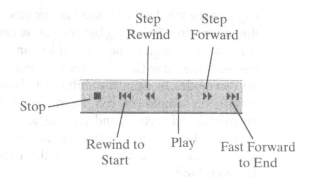

Figure 1.7 *The Controller Toolbar.*

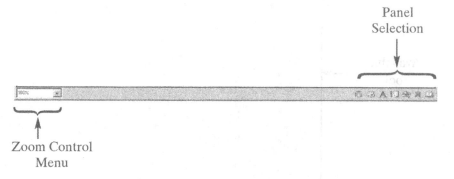

Figure 1.8 *The Launcher Bar.*

Next in the line is the Drawing Toolbar (referred to as the Toolbox by Macromedia). This has a set of tools which allow the user to create, select, paint and edit artwork, including text. As Figure 1.9 depicts, the Toolbar can be considered as having two parts: the tool section and the modifier section. Each tool has a set of modifiers linked with it. In chapter 2, we look at the application of some of these tools and what part the modifiers play. In fact, the rather innocent looking Toolbar has a powerful extension that provides much of the attraction in using Flash to create interactive and attractive artwork.

The positioning of the Drawing Toolbar can also be adjusted. It can be docked (that is, aligned with one of the two vertical edges of the window) or floated at any other position in the display window. Switching between these two modes can be performed through using the Ctrl key and left-clicking the mouse at the same time. Figures 1.10 and 1.11 demonstrate the two modes. By using the Shift key and single-clicking the mouse, the alignment can be made to toggle between horizontal and vertical, and vice versa. You can also toggle between the two positioning modes by simply double-clicking the mouse button when the cursor is over the Drawing Toolbar.

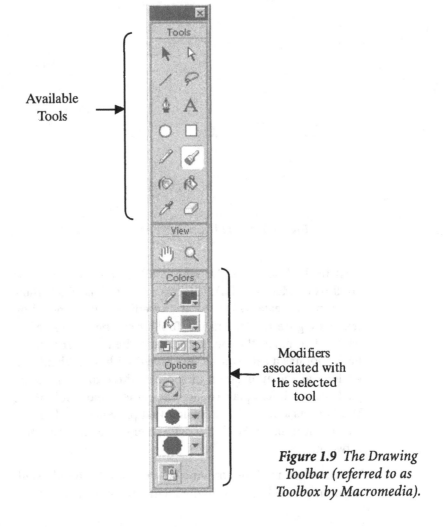

Available Tools

Modifiers associated with the selected tool

Figure 1.9 The Drawing Toolbar (referred to as Toolbox by Macromedia).

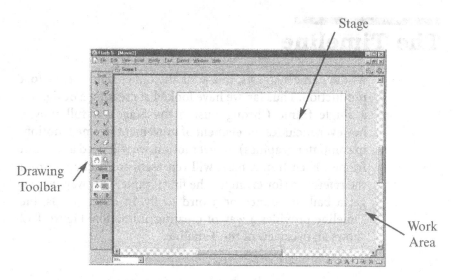

Figure 1.10 *The Drawing Toolbar horizontally docked at the left side vertical edge of the display window.*

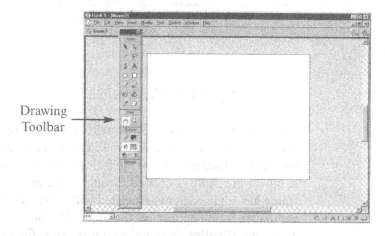

Figure 1.11 *The Drawing Toolbar floating horizontally close to the left edge of the display window.*

The Timeline

As the name suggests, this adds the dimension of time to a production. Thus far, we have looked at creating a design on a single frame (through using the Stage). A full movie, however, includes the element of movement (termed motion, in computer graphics). To get motion, we will need a series of frames. Each frame, here, will represent some change from the reference (for example, the first) frame. This way, we can get a ball to bounce or a bird to fly. In other words, the Timeline provides a way of creating animation. Figure 1.12 shows an overview of the Timeline.

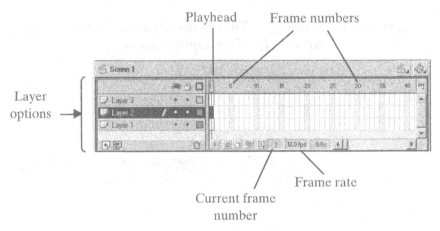

Figure 1.12 The Timeline.

There are several parts to the Timeline, most of which will be discussed in detail in chapter 9. The three sections that require mentioning now are the frames, playhead and layers. A movie normally is created through a set of frames. Each frame has some content associated with it. The contents of a particular frame appear on the Stage. The playhead moves across the Timeline, through the frames, and effectively plays the movie. The positioning of the playhead, at any one moment, is shown in the current frame number box (on the Timeline status line, see Figure 1.12). The frame number can also be read off directly from the Timeline header. Playing a movie would normally be undertaken by using the Controller Toolbar. By moving the playhead, however, the movie can be manually played. This is often useful for evaluating and debugging a production.

An important part of the Timeline is its inclusion of layers. When any artwork is created on the Stage, it is initially stored within a single layer. The artwork is then associated with the respective layer. This may be acceptable at the beginning of a project, but as more and more objects are placed on the artwork, it can become rather challenging to make changes and to edit. It is therefore recommended that more than one layer be used per frame. Multiple layers also provide the attraction of being able to add depth to an artwork. This way, objects can be positioned in terms of foreground and background. For example, placing a tree image in front of a house image can be done with two layers, where the top layer will have the tree image on it. It also allows the editing of one image without the worry of making unintentional changes to any other. The layers, in addition, provide an added dimension to creating attractive artwork. More on layers will be found in chapter 8.

The positioning of the Timeline can be done in a similar way to the Drawing Toolbar, where both modes of either floating or docking are available.

The Panels

The Flash environment provides a number of what Macromedia calls Panels. These effectively allow the user to view and edit parameters. There are a number of panels which can be activated. By choosing Window | Panels, a menu of panels appears. For example, if we wanted to inspect or to modify an artwork, we would use the window headed 'Info', which would offer us the following Panels:

- Info – size and position of selected objects (or instances of symbols)

- Transform – scale, rotate, skew objects (instances of symbols) or their copies
- Stroke – size and colour of strokes (outlines forming a shape)
- Fill – colour and texture (for example, solid, linear gradient, etc.).

Figure 1.13 shows the window headed 'Info'. The short-key associated with a window can be used as a toggle to switch on or off a desired Panel. The Panels, in fact, are grouped so that the 'Info' window contains Info, Transform, Stroke and Fill. It is possible to ungroup (then group) a respective Panel by simply moving it from (or to) the respective window through using their tabs. Figure 1.14 depicts this scenario. The application of Panels will be looked at in greater detail in subsequent chapters.

Options to manage Panels are also available. Under Windows, the following three can be used:

- Panel Sets – provides a list of all available (layout) sets that have been saved
- Save Panel Layout – stores the current panel layout as a set for future use
- Close All Panels – removes all panels from the application window.

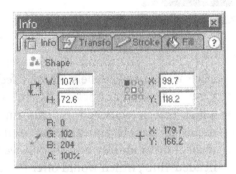

Figure 1.13 *The 'Info' window, consisting of the Panels: Info, Transform, Stroke and Fill.*

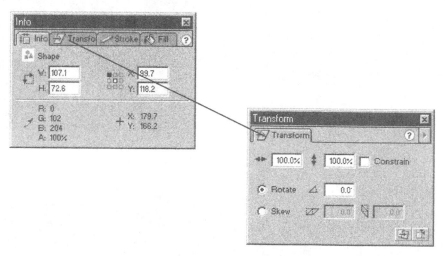

Figure 1.14 *The Transform Panel is ungrouped from the 'Info' window through using its tab. Other Panels can also have their own window, whilst regrouping is by moving respective Panels into a chosen window.*

Chapter 2

Flash Basics

Introduction

To make the best use of the working environment, it is important to grasp, at an early stage, some of the concepts and features that Flash offers. This way, we can customize the environment to suit our preference and requirements. In this chapter, we will extend our discussion of chapter 1 by looking at the topics listed below. Some of these will be looked at in greater detail in subsequent chapters:

- Bitmap and vector graphics
- Import and export of artwork
- Setting preferences
- Speeding-up displays
- Grids and rulers.

Bitmap and vector graphics

A graphical image can be represented by either a set of pixels or through a series of mathematical equations. In the case of the former, the representation is referred to as a bitmap. Here, the image is represented by display dots (for example, on some printers) or pixels. The pixels themselves are positioned within a grid framework to formulate an image. It is the intensity of each of the pixels that determines the contents of the display and therefore what image is created. The intensity can be monochrome (for example, black background with white foreground), or grey-shaded (with multiple increments going from black to white), or colour. In the case of the latter two, the number of grey levels and colours will depend on the available depth, that is, the number of bits that have been used to describe the intensity of the pixels. More on this can be found in chapter 6.

It may seem that the resulting output will only return a rough image (especially, if as it is likely, it consists of curved sections). The roughness (or, in other words, the smoothness) can, however, be controlled either through using high resolution output devices (therefore a lot more pixels per square inch) or applying some kind of anti-aliasing technique to reduce the impact of coarse outlines and edges. Figure 2.1 demonstrates the use of anti-aliasing to smooth the appearance of an edge.

Flash, however, by default uses vector graphics to represent images. By this, it is understood that, for example, instead of storing all the pixel positions for a straight edge, we simply save the coordinates for the end points and generate the edge on-the-fly. This concept is extended to cater for curved outlines by storing, in addition to the endpoints, a value for the respective curvature. In other words, mathematical expressions are employed for the description of an object, instead of their bitmaps.

What are the benefits of using vector graphics? There are a number of these, but the main three in the case of Flash are:

- Scalability of objects without distortion
- Size of files is relatively much smaller than bitmaps
- Transfer of object (i.e. files) over a network is much faster.

a)

b)

Figure 2.1 *Flash works by default with vector graphics and has also the feature of anti-aliasing which, as illustrated, smoothes the edges of an outline through using grey levels: (a) original outline, and (b) original with anti-aliasing.*

Import and export of artwork

Over a period of time, we will have generated, or have access to, a library of images which we may wish to import into a Flash movie. Moreover, we may be using a particular package (such as Adobe illustrator or Macromedia FreeHand) that we are familiar with to create graphics. If this is the case then it is reassuring to learn that Flash has an established means of accepting a number of image formats, whether they have been created as vectors or bitmaps.

By using File | Import, both vector and bitmap images can be imported into a Flash Movie. Table 2.1 lists the graphical file formats which can be imported into Flash 5.0.

Table 2.1 Graphical file formats accepted by Flash 5.0.

File Type	Extention
File Type	Extension
Adobe Illustrator	eps, ai
AutoCAD	dxf
Bitmap	bmp
Enhanced Windows Metafile	emf
Macromedia FreeHand	fh9,8,7 & ft9,8,7
FutureSplash Player	spl
GIF and animated GIF	gif
JPEG	jpg
PICT	pct, pic
PNG	png
Flash Player	swf
Windows Metafile	wmf

When a bitmapped image is imported, it is placed on the Stage and a copy is also stored in the Library. One benefit of having an object in the Library is that its instances can be used as desired. More on this and other features of the Library can be found in chapter 7. In the case of a vector image, when it is imported, it is placed on the Stage as a grouped object. Since the image is created from a series of vectors (for example, lines and curves), it needs to be ungrouped before any editing can take place on individual parts. Choose Modify | Ungroup to break the image down. Further discussion on importing bitmaps, including illustrative examples, is given in chapter 6.

Setting Preferences

Before commencing the creation of a Flash movie, it is worthwhile being aware of the defaults that have been set. These can be viewed and changed through using Edit | Preferences. Choosing this brings up in a dialogue box consisting of three tabs: General, Editing and Clipboard.

Figure 2.2 shows the options available under the General tab. These can be summarized as follows:

- Undo Levels – has a range of 0 to 200; the more levels, the higher the memory requirement
- Printing Options – usually deselect, unless you are having problems with printing to a PostScript printer
- Selection Options:
  - Shift Select – enabled requires the use of the Shift key to add objects to a selection; otherwise, objects can be added without the use of the Shift key
  - Show Tooltips – standard way of highlighting (via text box) a feature
- Timeline Options – Disable Timeline Docking when checked will separate the Timeline Window from the Application Window: the other two options are used to maintain similarity with Flash 4
- Highlight Color – use either palette to choose a colour or simply use the current layer colour
- Actions panel – use Expert to create action via ActionScript, otherwise use Normal to generate action through a set of controls.

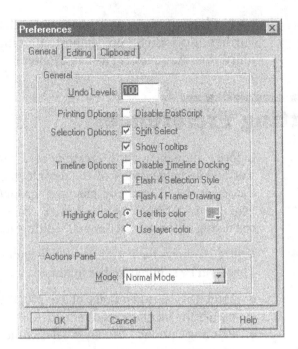

Figure 2.2 Preference tab for General settings.

As Figure 2.3 shows, the second Preference tab, headed Editing, provides a means of tailoring actions related to the Pen Tool and, probably more importantly, to the Drawing Settings. The Pen Tool will be looked at in greater detail in chapter 3. The Drawing Settings offer you the following five options:

- Connect lines – this is used by Flash to determine how close two lines have to be before they are considered to be connected. The parameter is also used for purposes of snapping objects together (via Snap to Objects option). In addition, it decides whether a line is horizontal (or vertical).
- Smooth curves – sets the smoothness of an outline drawn using the Pencil Tool
- Recognize lines – determines the level of straightness for Flash to recognize an outline as a line drawn by the Pencil Tool

- Recognize shapes – the parameter that allows Flash to establish a number of shapes such as a circle, oval, square, etc.
- Click accuracy – sets the distance to an object before Flash recognizes it
- Printing Options – usually deselect, unless you are having problems with printing to a printer.

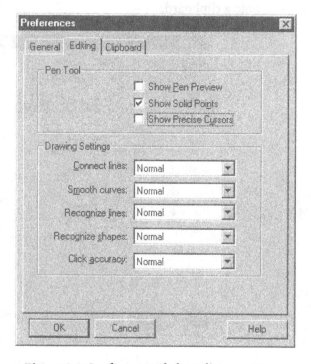

Figure 2.3 Preference tab for Editing settings.

The third setting which is grouped under the Preference menu is the Clipboard tab. This, as Figure 2.4 depicts, has a set of options which allows you to control the bitmaps that are placed on the clipboard. The four parameters can be described as follows:

- Color Depth – the number of bits to be used to describe the colour of the bitmap

- Resolution – the number of dots per inch to be used to establish the quality of the image
- Size limit – the amount of RAM to be employed for putting a bitmap onto a clipboard
- Smooth – provides anti-aliasing when checked.

The option labelled Quality (under Gradients) is useful when pasting Flash objects for use by another application. It determines the gradient quality of an object when pasted onto a clipboard.

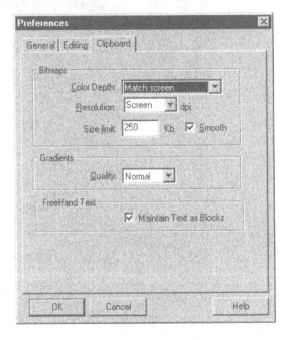

Figure 2.4 Preference tab for Editing settings.

Speeding-up displays

When producing a movie, especially one which contains a number of complex objects, it may be necessary to reduce the amount of computation to speed-up the displays. Flash allows you to control the amount of rendering required by making a selection through the View menu. The four relevant options are:

- Outlines – this is ideal for complex scenes since it only displays the outlines of objects and all lines appear as thin lines
- Fast – this displays all the colours and maintains the line styles of objects, but does not anti-alias any edges. This option is slower than the Outlines option, but is the most common mode
- Antialias – this allows for edges and shapes to appear smoother by allowing them to be anti-aliased by means of using a number of colour shades. This requires more computation than the first two options and thus is slower.
- Antialias Text – as the name suggests, this smoothes out the outlines of any text. Works best with large font sizes and can be slow with large amounts of text.

It should be noted that these options are applied to customize (that is, to control the speed and nature of) the display. They do not have any affect on how Flash will export the respective movie.

Grids, rulers and guides

Activating the grid in Flash results in a set of horizontal and vertical lines appearing on the Stage, behind any objects. These are used as guidelines for aligning and placing objects on the Stage or relative to each other. The grid itself is not exported as part of the final movie.

To activate the grid option, choose View | Grid. We can then select Show Grid. We may, however, choose to use the corresponding dialogue box by selecting (instead of Show Grid) Edit Grid. This results in the dialogue box shown in Figure 2.5. Here, we can choose to change the colour of the grid, the vertical and horizontal spacing of each grid cell, switch the grid on or off, have objects snapped to the grid and set the tolerance for snapping objects. In the case of the latter, we can choose from Must be close, Normal, Can be distant or Always snap. Note that, in Figure 2.5, the cell spacing is shown as pixels (px). This is in line with the measurements set for the Stage and, as such, can be changed using Modify | Movie and then Ruler Units. We also have the option of storing the type of grid for future use through the Save Default button.

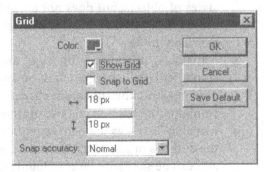

Figure 2.5 Dialogue box for the on-screen grid.

In addition to the grid, we have the option of using the ruler. Whilst the grid is useful for placing objects on the Stage, the ruler is great for positioning and sizing objects. When the ruler is activated by View | Ruler, vertical and horizontal sets appear as shown in Figure 2.6. Associated with the crosshair cursor on the Stage are corresponding markers on the ruler (see Figure 2.6) which indicate the cursor position with reference to the ruler measurements.

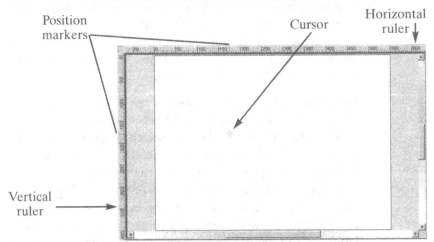

Figure 2.6 Using the ruler option allows for accurate positioning of objects by means of a marker placed on each of the two rulers.

Linked with the rulers is the option of activating guides. These provide for more precision through allowing for a series of horizontal and vertical lines to appear across the Stage. In a way, the properties of these lines (referred to as guides) are similar to the grid. We can change their colour, have objects snap to them and turn them on or off as desired, as well being able to decide on the tolerance before the object is snapped. The fundamental difference is that these allow us to manually set the positions so that they meet our desired production needs. For example, if we had created a bird as an object and wanted it to fly from point A on the Stage to point B, then we can precisely specify these points by means of the guides and have the bird snap to these points.

To insert a guide, simply move the cursor so it lies on top of either of the two rulers. Assuming we need a vertical guide, we position the cursor on the horizontal ruler. By pressing the left button, we should see the cursor shape change to that shown in Figure 2.7. By holding and dragging the mouse, we can then position the guide using the vertical ruler. The actual position will depend upon where we have released the mouse.

Figure 2.7 *The cursor changes shape to indicate that a vertical guide can be inserted on the Stage.*

The dialogue box and the set of options associated with guides comes under View | Guides. We can lock the guides so that they stay fixed on the Stage. Otherwise, they can be selected and re-positioned. To clear all guides or to save guides for future use, choose the corresponding options in the dialogue box.

Chapter 3

Simple Flash Objects

Introduction

Having established our environment, we are now ready to play and learn about the various features and tools that Flash provides to generate, manipulate and animate our artwork. In this chapter, we will learn more about the Toolbox and focus on the various tools that are available to us. The tools themselves look rather innocent in that they appear similar to other drawing packages. As we start to use them, however, we will soon see that creation and editing is done in a distinctive way – the Flash way. Naturally, early on, the full extent of the features may be difficult to grasp, but with more practice and experimentation, you will no doubt learn to appreciate the unique tools that Flash offers.

Tools on the Toolbox

The Flash 5 Toolbox looks somewhat different than the one available in earlier versions of Flash. It has two new tools, namely the Pen and the Subselect. The Toolbox is now sectionalized into four components: Tools, View, Colors and Options. Selecting a tool, will highlight whether there are any modifiers (such as filling or outline colour, the nature of the filling, etc.) associated with it. Figure 3.1 shows the Toolbox, together with the available tools.

It is important early on to grasp the difference between what is meant by a *stroke* and by a *fill*. Flash, like other drawing packages, makes extensive use of these and, more importantly, some of the modifiers are applicable to strokes, while others to fills. The basic difference can be illustrated through a simple everyday example. If we wanted to draw an apple tree on paper, then we would use a pencil to draw the outline shape (the trunk, the branches, the fruit, etc.). Having done this, we would probably then want to colour the trunk dark-brown, the branches brown and the apples red. We can do the same using Flash by, say, using the Pencil tool to draw the outlines (strokes) and using the Paint Bucket to add-in the colours (fills). As we tour the Toolbox, we will realize that some tools offer modifiers for both, whilst others only work with strokes or fills.

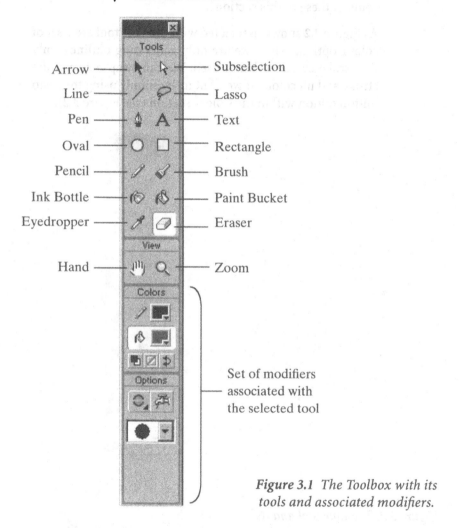

Arrow —— Subselection

Line —— Lasso

Pen —— Text

Oval —— Rectangle

Pencil —— Brush

Ink Bottle —— Paint Bucket

Eyedropper —— Eraser

Hand —— Zoom

Set of modifiers associated with the selected tool

Figure 3.1 *The Toolbox with its tools and associated modifiers.*

Drawing a straight line

The simplest tool to use to create objects on the Stage is the Line tool. This draws straight lines and can be used to produce artwork by connecting a series of lines together. Although the Line tool sounds innocent, its real contribution is only realized when you start to explore the number of add-on features that are associated with it. We will be looking at some of these in this section.

As Figure 3.2 shows, associated with the Line tool are a set of colour options. Since we are only generating outlines, only the stroke colour is being used. We can swap between the stroke and fill colour, if we want to, by simply using the swap button option within the Colors section (see Figure 3.2).

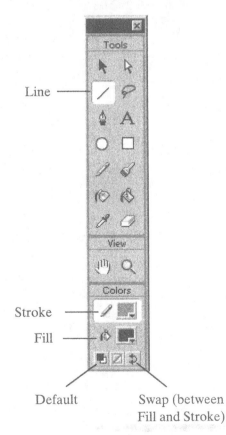

Figure 3.2 *The Line tool and its associated colour options.*

Default

Swap (between Fill and Stroke)

When the Line tool is selected, the cursor shape changes to that of a crosshair when placed anywhere on the Work Area or the Stage. In order to draw a line, simply position the cursor where you want the line to start and click (left mouse button) and drag it to its end point. A line will be drawn with reference to the current colour, type and thickness. We can also fix the orientation of the line to that of horizontal, vertical or at 45 degrees through using the Shift key whilst drawing.

If we wanted to change the attributes of the line, we simply use the Stroke panel (`Window | Panels`) to do this. As Figure 3.3 depicts, the panel will allow us to modify the type of line (for example, solid or dashed), its thickness and colour. Assuming we have already created a line, we would first use the Arrow tool to select it and then the panel to change the parameters. We can also customize the line to meet our desired requirements by choosing the Customise option. This will provide a dialogue box for us to work with. Any changes made to the line will be reflected in any new lines that are drawn.

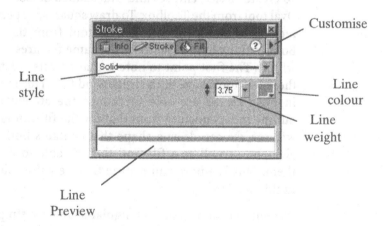

Figure 3.3 The Stroke panel with its various options.

Although we are generating outlines (that is, strokes), we can still choose to use the fill option. This may be useful if we wanted to add a gradient texture. The actual filling can be performed through the Fill panel. However, we first must transform our line so that this is permissible. Choose `Modify`

| Shape **and then** `Convert Lines to Fills` to activate the filling option. Figure 3.4 illustrates an example of how using the filling option can add impact to a line.

Normal

Converted to Fill

Figure 3.4 *Conversion to fills allows for the texture of the line to be filled using, as shown, a radial gradient.*

Drawing ovals and rectangles

To create circles, ellipses and oval shaped objects select the Oval tool from the Toolbox. To draw squares, trapezoids and rectangles choose the Rectangle tool from the Toolbox. Both options have essentially the same features associated with it. The first point to note is that objects created using these two tools have both strokes and fills. This means that, in practice, we are able to change the attributes of the outline independently from that for the fills. In fact, as we will see, we can draw a shape that contains both a stroke element, as well as a fill, and then be able to decompose them. This is a powerful feature that we will explore latter in this section.

To generate an oval or rectangular shape, we simply select the appropriate option from the Toolbox. Having done this, we should note that the cursor changes to a crosshair, as in the case of the Line tool. Drawing is done through selecting a position and dragging the mouse in the desired direction to produce an appropriately sized shape. For exact circles or squares, hold the Shift key down whilst drawing. Figure 3.5 depicts the creation of both an oval and rectangular shape.

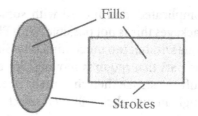

Fills

Strokes

Figure 3.5 Attributes of two objects created through using the Oval and Rectangle tools, respectively.

Both shapes could be drawn without their respective outlines or fills. The option within the Colors section (on the Toolbox) has a No Color button. This is shown in Figure 3.6. We can choose to have a circle, for example, without a fill and with just the outline, or vice versa.

Once a shape has been created, then the attributes discussed in the previous section (for the straight line case) are also applicable here for the stroke and fill.

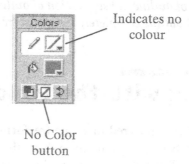

Indicates no colour

No Color button

Figure 3.6 By selecting the No Color button, we can choose between whether we wish the oval or rectangular shape to possess a stroke or a fill or both. In the example shown, we only want the fill and not the stroke.

Assume that we have created a circle with both stroke and fill features so that there is an outline, as well as a coloured interior. We may now wish to decompose the circle so that the outline is separated from the interior fill. This sounds complicated, and indeed with some drawing and graphics packages this is not possible. With Flash, however, this can be done without too much difficulty. Simply place the cursor on the part that requires moving. For example, if we wanted to shift the stroke then the cursor needs to be on top of this. A single mouse click will then select this (and not the fill). We can then choose to re-position the stroke, leaving the fill (which still is a circle) untouched. Figure 3.7 animates the process. We would do the same if we wanted the filled interior to be moved. Note that, to select the whole object, we will need to double-click (instead of single click) on the filled area.

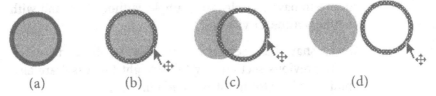

(a)   (b)   (c)   (d)

Figure 3.7 Decomposition of a filled circle with an outline: (a) original, (b) selection of outline, (c) separation of outline from filled interior, and (d) outline completely separated from filled interior.

Drawing with the Pencil tool

Often referred to as the freeform tool, it allows us to create artwork very similar to that using a pencil to draw on paper. Unlike some other graphics packages, however, the Flash environment has some unique features that converts the rough edged drawing into either a smooth (curved) outline or one consisting of straight lines. We can, of course, work without these so that your artwork is not smoothed or straightened by choosing to work in the Ink (freeform) mode. The combination with the Shift key ensures that lines are either horizontal or vertical.

Once the Pencil tool is selected, within the Options section of the Toolbox, a menu can be opened and an appropriate choice concerning the type of feature (straighten, smooth or ink) can be made. Figure 3.8 gives an illustration of this.

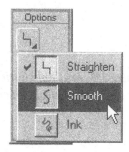

Figure 3.8 Artwork created using the Pencil tool can be assisted so that lines appear straight (Straighten) or curved (Smooth); otherwise the freehand mode can be used (Ink).

Having used the Pencil tool to generate artwork, the outline style (line type, colour, size, etc.) can be changed by using the Stroke panel or through converting the outlines to fills (Modify | Shape and then Convert Lines to Fills) and using the Fill panel.

Flash also allows for the outlines to be further smoothed or straightened even after they have been created. If there is a need to do this, then simply select the Arrow tool and double-click on the artwork produced using the Pencil tool. You should then see five buttons appear in the Options section of the Toolbox. This is shown in Figure 3.9. The same options are also on the Main Toolbar (see Figure 1.6).

As mentioned in chapter 2 under 'Setting Preferences', the degree of assistance can be adjusted to meet a desired or specified tolerance. In other words, when to recognize that a Pencil drawn outline is a line, or that two lines can be considered to be connected or the level of smoothness to apply to curved outlines.

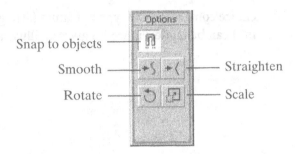

Figure 3.9 Available options for further adjustments to artwork that has been created using the Pencil tool.

Drawing with the Brush tool

Instead of using a pencil to create our artwork, we may want to use a set of brush strokes to do the same. Of course, we have the choice of drawing an outline using the Pencil and then filling it manually through the application of the Brush tool. This may sound a bit involved as it is always difficult to keep the paint inside an outline, but we will see that this is well catered for by Flash.

The selection of the Brush tool results in three modes being available within the Options section of the Toolbox. These refer to the size of the brush, its shape and the type of filling required. Figure 3.10 shows the corresponding Options section.

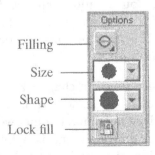

Figure 3.10 Options available when the Brush tool is selected.

The shape of the cursor that appears on the Stage (and on the Work Area) depends on the Shape and Size that has been selected. In other words, it reflects both of these parameters. What may be more interesting is that the shape can be changed so that it mirrors a calligraphic pen. Figure 3.11 illustrates this point, where the brush working in this mode is used to generate some writing in the Arabic language (which is known for its calligraphic style). We will be looking at the filling modes of the Brush tool in greater detail in chapter 4.

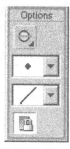

Figure 3.11 The Brush tool in the mode shown has been used to write my (first) name in a calligraphic style using the Arabic language.

Working with the Pen tool

The primary purpose of this tool is to provide better precision when creating line or curve segments, or complete outlines making use of a series of these segments. To understand this better, we need to be aware firstly that lines are generated through a set of two end points (Flash refers to these as anchor points). In other words, a line is defined by simply specifying the positions of the two end points. When we select the Pen tool to draw a line, we specify the first end point by positioning the crosshair cursor on the desired location and then we re-position for the second end point. Note that we are not clicking and dragging here. If we then wanted to add another line segment, then we simply specify another end point. A new line will be drawn from this point to the previous end point that was specified. Figure 3.12 demonstrates the process. These lines can be converted to fills as with those drawn with the Pencil tool.

Drawing curved segments is a little more involved, though it too makes use of the previously drawn segment. A curve segment consists of two end points and a couple of what are called control points. The purpose of the control points is to determine the shape of the curve, together with specifying the slopes at the two respective end points. Figure 3.13 depicts this scenario. To create a curve segment, we would need to click the mouse and then drag it to form our desired shape.

a)   b)

Figure 3.12 The use of the Pen tool to create line segments: (a) first line with crosshair specifying the end point of second line, and (b) generation of second line with reference to the first line end point.

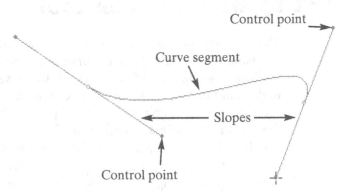

Figure 3.13 Generation of a curved segment using the Pen tool is undertaken through defining the two end points and the two control points.

Chapter 4

Editing Flash Objects

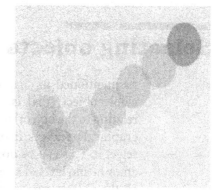

Introduction

One of the treats in using Flash is the versatility it offers when it comes to editing objects. It incorporates the traditional cut, copy and paste operations, together with a number of other features that allows for smooth alterations necessary for working with artwork. Often, when we create a scene, we may only want to make minor adjustments that meet a desired look. This could be in the form of adding a background, for example, to a ball bouncing across the screen, or creating a shadow for the ball, or changing its texture, or even the shape of the ball to reflect a particular sport. In addition we could decompose the ball (that is, divide it into several sections) to produce a picture that showed the ball being used as a vase for some flowers. Strange as it may sound, but this is all possible with some of the sophisticated tools that Flash offers. Moreover, Flash works with vectors so there is usually no loss of quality when working with sub-sections of an artwork. In this chapter, we look at some of the tools and features available to us for editing images on the Stage.

Selecting objects

As mentioned in chapter 3, Flash has a way of selecting a whole object (that is, one that contains all the attributes relating to the object) or just sections of an object. Like other graphical packages, in order to edit an artwork, we must first select it. This can be done in several ways, depending on the amount and level of selection required. If we wanted to select all the objects currently on the Stage, for example, then we could simply choose to use Edit | Select All. Using the Arrow tool will allow us to select particular objects (and sub-sections), whilst the Lasso tool works as with other packages where a number of objects can be chosen by identifying a particular area of the Stage. If we wanted to make finer adjustments or even change the shape of created objects then the Subselection tool can assist us. Figure 4.1 shows the positioning of these tools on the Toolbox and the following sections provide an insight to how these tools could be used.

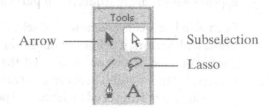

Figure 4.1 Three tools that offer various levels of object selection.

Using the Arrow tool

The Arrow tool is the one commonly used for selecting objects. When activated, it offers four types of selection:

- Both outline and fill
- Outline only
- Fill only
- Marquee (usually more than one object).

If we take the example of a square with a filled area as shown in Figure 4.2, it can be seen that we can choose to select an edge, all four edges, the filled area or the whole object. To select an edge, we simply place the cursor on the edge and click once. For all four edges, we will need to click twice. The filled area can be selected by a single click; clicking twice will result in the whole object being selected.

What if we wanted to select only two of the edges? This is not a problem. Depending upon the preference settings, we can either Shift-click or simply click the second edge to select it. As mentioned in chapter 2, we will find this setting under Edit | Preferences, and then General.

Marquee selection is where a rectangular area is used to define an area containing parts of an object, or the whole object, or more than one object. It is typically used for the latter. Figure 4.3 depicts this case. The Shift-click can be used to add to this selection. Care must be taken when working with this mode since it selects everything that appears within the marquee, even parts of an object.

Flash also has a convenient way of selecting outlines. Since it works with vectors, it defines an outline in terms of curves and lines. When the Arrow tool is selected, the cursor can be used to identify (and modify) between a curve outline and a corner point (the latter being used to define end points for curves and lines). An arc or a right-angle icon is appended to the cursor arrow to indicate the type. Figure 4.4 shows an example of both cases. Modification in both cases is performed (whilst the icon is appended to the cursor) through click and drag.

As vectors are being used, an outline will consist of a number of segments. To select more than one segment using either the arc or right-angle icon appended cursor, we simply use the Shift key or click on the appropriate segment (as described above).

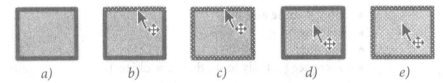

a)   b)   c)   d)   e)

Figure 4.2 *Various levels of selection: (a) original, unselected object, (b) top edge selected using a single click, (c) outline (four edges) selected using double click, (d) filled area selected using a single edge, and (e) the whole object selected through using two clicks.*

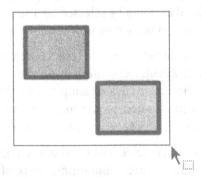

Figure 4.3 *Marquee selection (click and drag) being used to select two objects.*

Using the Lasso tool

The Lasso tool is used to select objects that may have an odd shape or where two objects are so close to each other as to require a manual selection. The tool works like in other graphics packages in that it allows for an area on the Stage to be selected. This does not necessarily result in a complete object being selected, but returns only those parts which fall within the selection. Figure 4.5 gives an illustration of this, where the Lasso tool is in freehand mode and the selection area is defined through the standard click and drag operation. It is not necessary to define a closed area, since Flash will automatically use a straight line to make a loop.

Figure 4.6 depicts the three buttons associated with the Lasso tool. These appear under the Options section on the Toolbox. The Polygon Mode modifier works with defining a straight edge selection area. Simply through single clicking, end points for the lines are specified. Double-clicking closes the selection area. Figure 4.7 gives an illustration of the Lasso tool in this mode.

It is possible to work in both freehand and straight edge selection modes. Deselect the Polygon Mode modifier to use freehand. To draw a straight edge segment, use the Alt key with the mouse to define end points for the edges. Selection areas can be closed either by releasing the mouse (freehand)

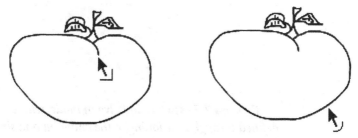

Figure 4.4 Identification and modification of either a corner (edge, line) section or a curve segment can be undertaken by placing the cursor near the outline, whilst using the Arrow tool.

or double-clicking (straight edge). In addition, the Lasso tool has two other modifiers: Magic Wand and Magic Wand Settings. In chapter 6, we look at the role of these two modifiers and show how these can be used to select and change the properties of bitmaps.

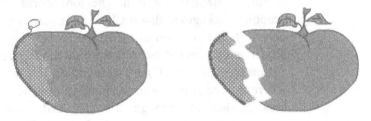

Figure 4.5 Through using the Lasso tool, a desired area of an object on the Stage can be selected.

Figure 4.6 Lasso tool works with three modes (Magic Wand, Magic Wand Settings,and Polygon) which are available in the Options section of the Toolbox.

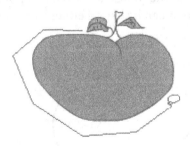

Figure 4.7 Lasso tool in Polygon mode, where an area is defined through positioning of the endpoint and single clicking. The lines are connected together in a piecewise manner. Double clicking will complete the process and Flash will automatically connect the last point with the first by a straight line.

Using the Brush tool

The Brush tool, as the name suggests, behaves like an everyday brush where it can be used to draw outlines, as well as perform manual fills. The latter can take the form of colours, gradients and bitmaps. Apart from having a variety of brush sizes and shapes, it has five modes of (filling) operations which provide a powerful way of creating realistic artistic effects. As Figure 4.8 depicts, a filling type can be selected using the Brush Mode button located in the Options section of the Toolbox.

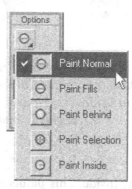

Figure 4.8 The menu showing the five operational modes for the Brush tool available within the Options section of the Toolbox when the Brush tool is active.

With reference to the examples shown in Figure 4.9, the five modes of operation can be summarized as follows:

- Paint Normal. This will paint over strokes and fills belonging to objects on the same layer.
- Paint Fills. This will paint only interiors of outlines (that is, fills), leaving the strokes unaffected.
- Paint Behind. This will not affect the fills or the strokes of the objects, but it will paint the background to the object.
- Paint Selection. This will paint interiors of outlines (that is, fills) which have been selected. It does not affect the strokes.

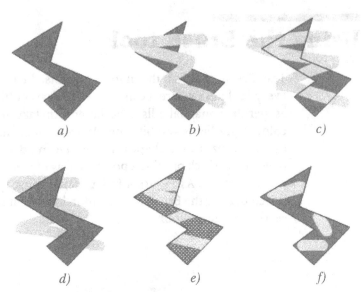

Figure 4.9 *This shows the working of the modes for the Brush tool: (a) original, (b) Paint Normal, (c) Paint Fills, (d) Paint Behind, (e) Paint Selection (note that the fill is highlighted), and (f) Paint Inside.*

- Paint Inside. This paints interiors only when the brush stroke starts from a filled region. It leaves the strokes unaffected.

If we wanted to restrict the movement of the brush to the horizontal and vertical then we would combine the click and drag with the Shift key.

Using the Paint Bucket tool

Often it becomes necessary to not just change the shape of an object, but also the colour or texture of its filled areas. The Paint Bucket tool comes into play when this is required. This tool can fill complete enclosures, as well as outlines containing gaps. The size of the gaps can be controlled in that filling takes place in reference to this (see below).

To fill an outline with a colour (or to change the fill colour), select the Paint Bucket tool from the Toolbox. Under the Colors section, choose the desired colour from the pop-up menu. Figure 4.10 gives an illustration of this. Having chosen an appropriate colour, place the (bucket) cursor over the fill area and single click. This will fill enclosed outlines and not necessary the whole object. For example, if your object is in the form of a star (drawn using the pencil tool), then it will contain six sections. Each section is treated differently and can thus have different colours. Figure 4.11 depicts the scenario. To fill the whole object, select the object using the Arrow tool and then choose colour as with Paint Bucket.

Associated with the Paint Bucket tool is a set of modifiers. These can be found under the Options section on the Toolbox. These provide a way of controlling the filling process for outlines that are not completely enclosed. The modifiers are shown in Figure 4.12. If the gaps are too large, then the shape will require adjustment to allow filling to take place. Also, the zooming feature has no effect on the actual size of the gap. More discussion on colours and gradients can be found in chapter 6.

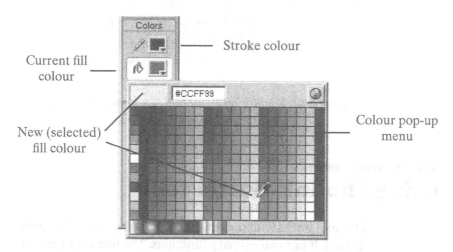

Figure 4.10 Fill colours for the Paint Bucket tool are chosen via a pop-up menu as shown.

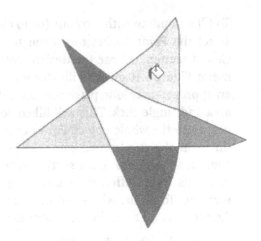

Figure 4.11 The use of the Paint Bucket tool to fill affects only enclosed sections forming an object. In the example, the six sections are filled using different colours.

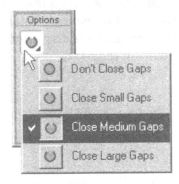

Figure 4.12 The Bucket Paint tool can be set to treat gaps within enclosures as required.

Using the Ink Bottle tool

This tool works with the outlines of the artwork (rather than its fills). It has two primary functions. The first is to provide an outline for a fill that does not already have one. The colour, thickness and style used for this will depend on the current settings on the Stroke panel. The colour can also be chosen using the Colors section on the Toolbox. When the Ink Bottle tool is activated, choose the desired colour from the pop-up menu associated with the stroke colour (see Figure 4.10). An example of the Ink Bottle tool being used to generate an outline is given in Figure 4.13.

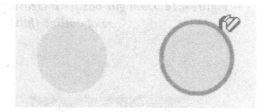

Figure 4.13 *The use of the Ink Bottle tool to produce an outline for a filled area.*

Its second and more prominent purpose is to facilitate the modification of attributes associated with the outline. One of these, obviously, is the colour. The others are linked to the stroke style (for example, thickness). Strokes cannot usually have fills apart from colour. It is not directly possible, for example, to fill a stroke with a gradient. Flash, however, has the option of converting lines into fills. As mentioned in chapter 3, the option Modify | Shape, and then Convert Lines to Fills makes this possible. The outline can, in addition, be made to appear swollen or shrunk. This is achieved through a process referred to as expanding (sometimes called contouring). To activate this, we need to convert the lines to fills and then choose Modify | Shape, Expand Fill. This opens the dialogue box shown in Figure 4.14. Here, the Distance refers to the number of pixels that will be involved in the process of expansion or reduction, with reference to the outside edge. The range for the distance is 0.05–144 pixels. The Direction says whether an expansion (Expand) or reduction (Inset) is required.

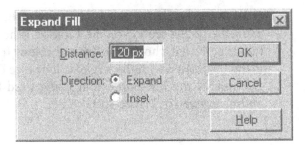

Figure 4.14 *Dialogue box for increasing and reducing the size of outline (fills).*

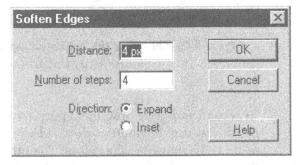

Figure 4.15 *Dialogue box for blurring (softening) edges.*

Another option associated with the outlines is blurring the edges. This is referred to as softening the edges since the overall effect is to make the outlines appear smoother and thus more pleasing to the eye. To activate this option select Modify | Shape and then Soften Fill Edges. This results in the dialogue box shown in Figure 4.15. The settings are similar to the ones belonging to the Expand Fill, apart from the fact that these now refer to the soft edge effect rather than expanding outlines. The notable difference is the Number of steps. This specifies the amount of smoothness required. A high value here (for example, 15 onwards) results in a softer edge. The price one pays for this is that this needs a lot of processing power. As a consequence, the quality of the playback will suffer since a lot of calculation is required to generate an image. So, in practice, an equilibrium will need to be established between smoothness and the amount of processing power required.

Using the Eraser tool

This tool works similarly to other graphics packages in that it permits the removal of lines, fills and shapes. These can be as a whole or partial. The eraser can take on a number of shapes, it can be set to erase outlines or fills only, and can work in deleting complete or partial segments.

There are three modifiers available for this tool: Eraser Shape, Eraser Mode and Faucet. The positioning of these within the Options section of the Toolbox is shown in Figure 4.16. There are 10 basic shapes that the Eraser works with. These are shown in Figure 4.17.

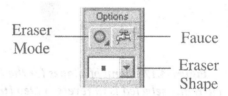

Figure 4.16 *Modifiers for the Eraser tool.*

Once a shape for the Eraser is determined, the exact way of operation will depend on the current mode settings. As Figure 4.18 depicts, there are five modes. The working of these is as follows:

- Normal – erases strokes and fills as per other graphical packages
- Erase Fills – deletes fills only
- Erase Lines – deletes strokes only
- Erase Selected Fills – deletes only fills that have been selected
- Erase Inside – deletes only the fill within which the eraser process began.

The Faucet option is really a shorthand way of deleting lines or fills. When this is activated, the cursor changes to resemble the Faucet icon. A line or fill can be deleted by simply placing the Faucet hot spot (the drop of water) on the segment that requires to be deleted. A single mouse click would then erase the segment (whether fill or outline). It works similarly to the process of selecting a segment, then using the Delete key.

Figure 4.17 Menu of shapes for the Eraser tool. The one currently selected is in reverse video (the third from the top).

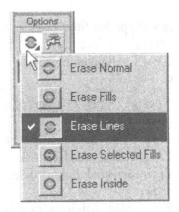

Figure 4.18 The five modes for the Eraser tool.

Using the Dropper tool

As we begin to develop our design, the artwork will become more and more complex. Attempting to make only minor changes can be difficult. The Dropper tool can be a handy feature which could be used at any phase of development, but more so when the complexity of the production demands certain features (for example, colour, line style, etc.) to be known or to be shared by other objects.

When the Dropper tool is selected, the attributes of an outline can be sampled by positioning the respective cursor over it and using a single click. When this happens, the tool automatically changes to the Ink Bottle tool. This is reflected in the change of tool on the Toolbox and the shape of cursor to that of an Ink Bottle. Figure 4.19 gives an example of this.

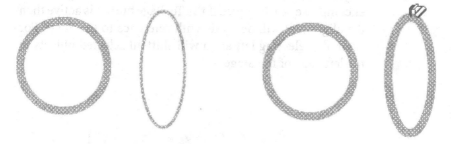

Figure 4.19 The attributes of the circle are shared by the ellipse by means of the Dropper tool, which automatically changes to a Ink Bottle tool once the original has been sampled.

The process with fills is the same in that the original is sampled and its attributes can be viewed and shared by other objects. In this case, however, the tool (and thus the cursor) that it switches to after the sample is the Paint Brush.

Aligning objects

Having created a series of objects, it is often necessary to place these on the Stage within a desired layout. Using the Snap to Grid and Snap to Guidelines (see chapter 2) can assist us in this process whereby objects are laid out with reference to the Grid and Guides. In addition, there are a number options that allow alignment either with reference to other objects or to the Stage. Some of these options are unique to Flash.

To activate the alignment dialogue box, choose Window | Panels and then Align. Clicking the appropriate button available on the Main Toolbar can also open the same menu (see Figure 1.6: the Align button is the last button on the right). The corresponding panel is shown in Figure 4.20. The first row of options (headed Align) are commonly found in other graphical packages. With these, objects can be aligned to each other through left, centre or right edges. They can also be aligned with reference to the top, middle and bottom edges. The alignment is with respect to the bounding box that encompasses each object. If the To Stage button is active then the alignment will be made with reference to the Stage. For example, selecting left align will shift all selected objects to the left edge of the Stage.

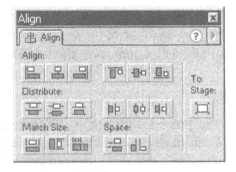

Figure 4.20 Alignment dialogue box.

The set of options available under Distribute refers to the spacing between objects. The spacing is made the same (even) between objects either vertically (top, middle, bottom) or horizontally (left, centre, right).

If there was a need to scale an object or a set of objects to match each other, then there is a convenient option under Match Size that makes this available. The object's width, height or both can be scaled to match.

Using the two Space buttons, objects can, for example, be evenly spaced with reference to differing edges, so that for vertical alignment, the bottom edge of the first object is spaced with the top edge of the second object.

Transformation of objects

Additional features to modify artwork can be found within the panel headed Transform. These include the option of scaling, rotating and skewing. Having selected an object or objects, we can activate the panel through Window | Panels, and then Transform. This results in the panel shown in Figure 4.21. We select and enter values for the desired transformation. The option of Constrain next to the scaling row can be used to match both horizontal and vertical values. This provides for uniform scaling. As Figure 4.21 shows, the entered values can be reset and the transformation can be applied to a copy of the selected objects rather than to the originals. The effect of the transformation is applied (and thus can be viewed on the Stage) once the Return/Enter key is pressed.

The common rotate and scale features, in fact, are also available via the Options section of the Toolbox when the Arrow tool is active or through the Main Toolbar. In addition, choosing Modify | Transform opens a sub-menu which can be used to modify selected objects. Figure 4.22 gives an illustration of this and the set of available options. Some of these will be discussed in later chapters.

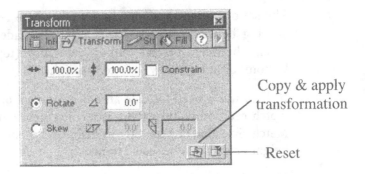

Figure 4.21 Transform Panel.

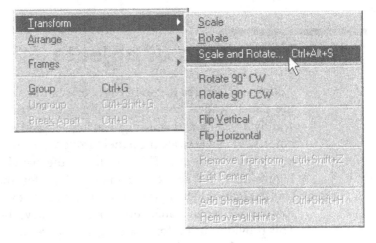

Figure 4.22 Available transformation options through
Modify | Transform.

Chapter

5

Adding Text

Introduction

Thus far we have looked at working with artwork, the basics of creating an image and then being able to use the tools and features of Flash to fine-tune it so it meets the desired requirements. Although graphical images can suffice for some particular types of design, the addition of text often clarifies and amplifies the message that is being promoted. It is sometimes difficult looking an animation to comprehend its real meaning, or at least the meaning the designer had in mind. To overcome this situation, the use of text (even one word) can provide enough navigation for the user to appreciate the significance of the animation.

Working with text in Flash, as you may expect, takes on a new significance. We can write a short description like a word-processor, apply some transitions like fading in or out, animate it to produce a banner for example and, probably more importantly, apply the text either in active or interactive mode. The latter includes editable text boxes where input data could be entered and displayed. The form of these could be user surveys, or something more dynamic. Examples of the latter include share prices, sports scores, weather reports, etc. In this chapter, we will look at these and other features through exploring the generation and use of Flash text.

Understanding Flash text

Clearly, Flash is an animation package and not a word-processor. So the options to work with text are limited in comparison but are unique to generating applications suitable for the web. Text can be sized, have its colour and typeface changed, be more or less spaced and can also be aligned. The transformations mentioned in chapter 4 for graphics can also be applied to text. So we can rotate, scale, skew and flip individual characters, or a group of characters, a word, a sentence or a paragraph. Moreover, we can still edit the text even after it has been transformed. In addition to having dynamic text boxes, we can also link our text to URLs, and have our typed text spell-checked.

If we prefer, we can have Flash treat our text as shapes instead of characters and words. This then opens up a number of additional options in the form of being able to change the appearance (for example, shape) and the look of text. Later in this chapter, we will discuss this further through some examples and illustrations.

Using the Text tool

The Text tool on the Toolbox (see Figure 3.1), when activated, allows for text be placed on the Stage. The cursor changes to that of a crosshair with the appended letter A. We then have a choice of deciding whether to create (what is referred to as) a text label or a text block. The former is simply where we may want to enter a line of text. The length of the line is dynamic so it increases as more text is entered. Using text blocks, on the other hand, results in a fixed width so that the height of the block is increased on-the-fly to match the amount of text.

The attributes for the text can be changed through using three panels: Character, Paragraph and Text Options. The Character panel is shown in Figure 5.1. Here, the typeface for the character (for example, Times New Roman, Arial, Impact, etc.), the colour, size, spacing between characters (including kerning), style (bold, italicize, superscript and subscript) and a URL link can be specified. More on this is given later in this chapter.

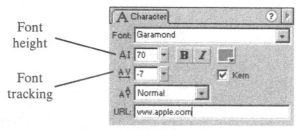

Figure 5.1 The Character panel provides for some standard set of modifiers for text, as well as the option of linking the selected text to a specified URL.

The Paragraph panel, on the other hand, facilitates text alignment, left and right margin settings, indentation and line spacing. The corresponding panel is shown in Figure 5.2.

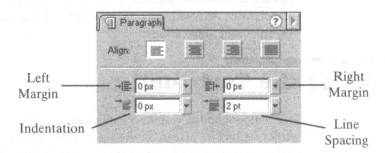

Figure 5.2 The Paragraph panel.

The third panel, Text Options, is mainly used for dynamic and input text. It allows control over the nature of the appearance of such text in a Flash movie. Figure 5.3 depicts the respective panel. As can be seen from this there are a number of options available. The main option is whether we wish to create dynamic text (one that automatically changes) or input text (one that requires user involvement). Both make use of an editable box. This is discussed in the next section, whilst the discussion on dynamic and input text can be found in chapter 10 (Interactivity and Scripting).

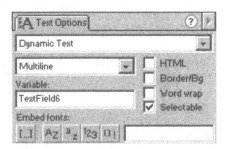

Figure 5.3 Panel for working with dynamic and input text.

Working with text

To produce a piece of text (often referred to as a block), whether single or multiline, we activate the Text tool. Before creating any text, we may want to open the Character and Paragraph panels to view what the current settings are. We can open these either through the previously mentioned Window | Panels route, or the dedicated Text menu. In the latter case, we would open the panels by selecting Text | Character and Text | Paragraph, respectively. Changes to attributes can be made prior to creating text or after some text has been written (where in this case the text will need to be selected and then attributes applied to it).

Flash works with text blocks, whether a single line label is being created or a passage is being produced. The way text appears within the block is established through the shape of the handles that are used to distinguish between expand (that is, single line, flexible length) and fixed (where the length of the line is set, but can have multiple lines) text modes. The appropriate handle appears in the top right corner of the text box.

Working in the expand mode, the handle shape takes the form of a small circle. This is shown in Figure 5.4, where we can also see the length of the text box changing to accommodate the text label.

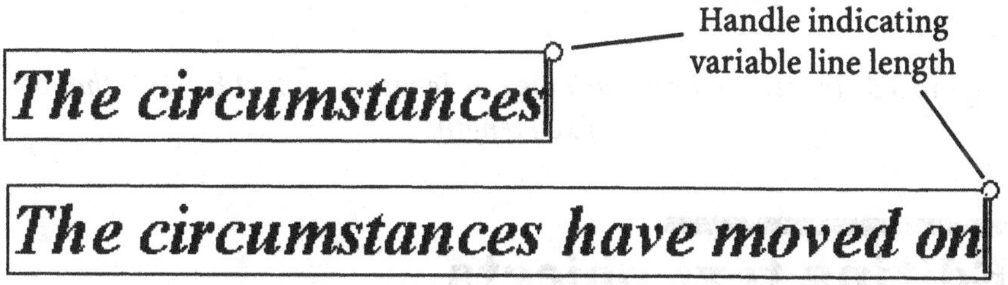

Handle indicating
variable line length

The circumstances

The circumstances have moved on

Figure 5.4 Producing text labels through using the expand mode for the text block, where the text box increases its size to cater for the corresponding increase in text.

In the fixed mode, we follow the steps as described above to activate the text option. Before writing any text, however, we define the length of the lines through dragging the handle to an appropriate (size) position. When this happens, the handle changes shape to that of a square to indicate that the block of text has a fixed length and that any text not fitting this length will be wrapped onto the next line. Figure 5.5 illustrates the workings of this mode.

It is also possible to have multiple lines within the variable length mode. In this case, we would simply insert line breaks (through using the Enter or Return key) at the desired places. We can also view text that goes beyond the Stage by choosing View | Work Area. If the text handle is still not visible, then the text block will need to be moved. This is done through either using the Arrow (selection) tool or by selecting the text whilst in Text mode. In both cases, we click and drag the text block so that the resizing handle becomes visible.

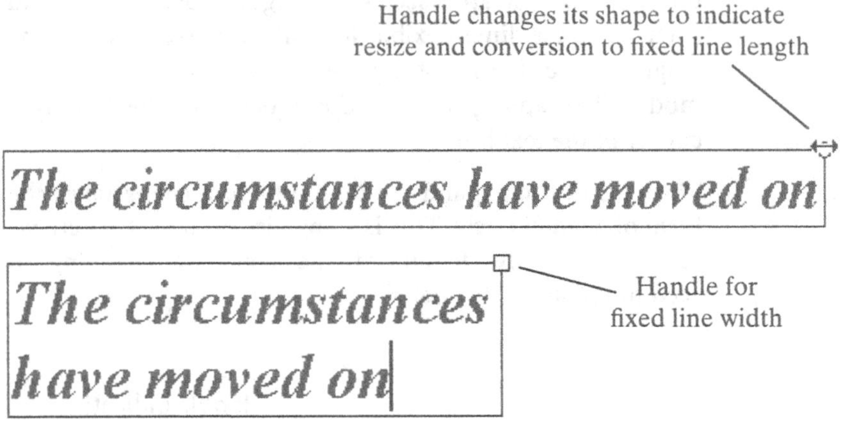

Handle changes its shape to indicate
resize and conversion to fixed line length

The circumstances have moved on

The circumstances
have moved on

Handle for
fixed line width

Figure 5.5 *Transition from variable line length for a text block to that of fixed length.*

Editing text objects

Having created a text block, we may want to fine-tune it so that it meets our desired objective. There are a number of ways that we could proceed. The first point to note is that the environment supports the common features of cut, copy and paste. This is true for artwork as well as text. In addition, we can rotate and align text. The editing process can be performed on whole blocks, or on individual characters. As we will see in this section, the way Flash allows for this is similar to some degree to working on a word-processor.

Let us assume that we wish to edit a text block as a whole. We select the corresponding text through using the Arrow tool. A single mouse click will select the relevant text, whilst double clicking will take you to text editing mode. In the former case, the text block becomes an object (a text object) whose attributes can be modified. The latter case, on the other hand, results in the appearance of the text editing cursor within the text block, in addition to the mode handle. This then facilitates any corrections or adjustments that maybe required to the original text. Figure 5.6 illustrates both cases.

Although it may not be clear from Figure 5.6, the box surrounding the text object case (Figure 5.6(a), cyan in the example shown) is of a different colour to that of the editing case (Figure 5.6(b)). The process of selecting more than one text block is similar to that of graphical objects. We combine text blocks either through the combination of the Shift key and click or simply by clicking (this depends on the preference setting) the desired blocks. Like graphical objects, text blocks can be assembled together via Modify | Group. Figure 5.7 depicts this scenario.

This way, we can apply attributes to grouped text objects. Figure 5.8 illustrates the case for scaling. Here, we have scaled the text using the bottom left handle through the click and drag process. This feature becomes available within the Options section of the Toolbox once the text object is selected using the Arrow tool. In a similar manner, the text object can be rotated using the respective feature within the Options section.

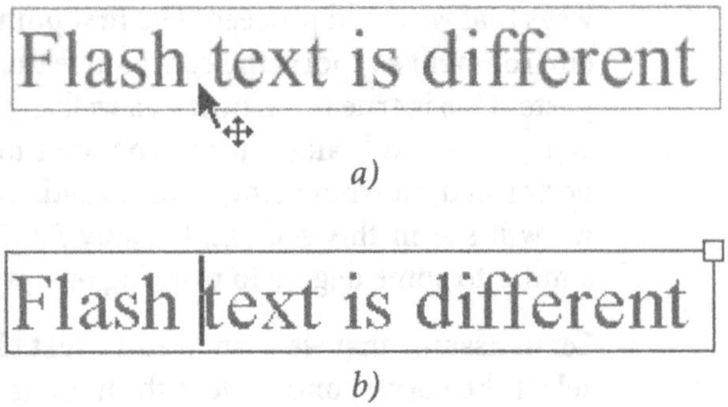

Flash text is different

a)

Flash text is different

b)

Figure 5.6 *Selection of text block: (a) single mouse click results in the text being treated as an object, and (b) double click results in entering text editing (insertion, correction, etc.) mode.*

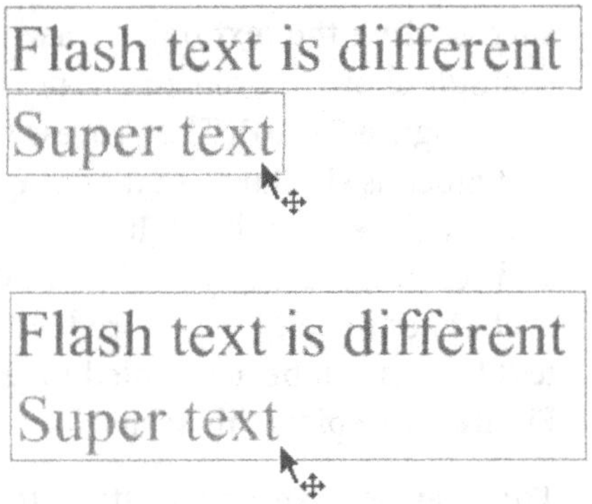

Flash text is different
Super text

Flash text is different
Super text

Figure 5.7 *Combining two blocks of text, via* `Modify | Group`.

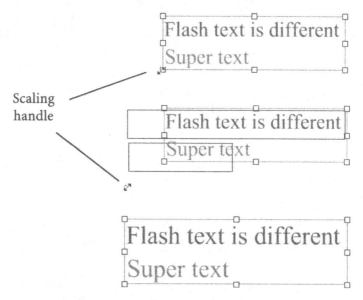

Figure 5.8 Resizing of a text object by choosing a resizing handle (bottom left in the above example) and dragging it to give the desired size.

Figure 5.9 depicts an animated example of this. Note that the resultant text object still has a rectangular bounding box surrounding it. Rotation is performed using the four corner handles of the bounding box. The other four (referred to as centre) handles cater for skewing, where both horizontal and vertical skewing can be applied. Figure 5.10 shows an example of how an object can be skewed.

Corner
(rotation)

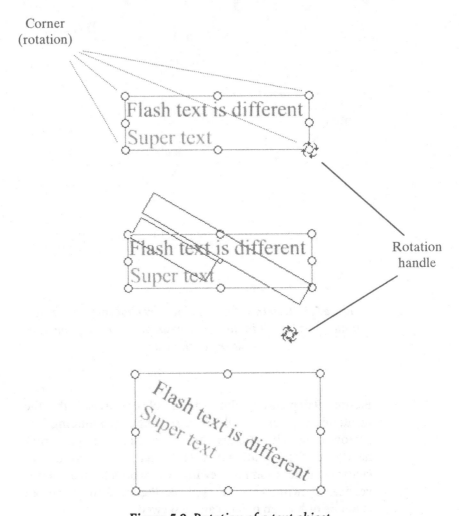

Rotation
handle

Figure 5.9 Rotation of a text object.

Instead of clicking and dragging handles to perform transformations, we can use the Transform panel to precisely specify the amount of rotation or skewing desired. Choose Window | Panels and then Transform to activate this option. To set values for both rotation and scaling simultaneously, choose Modify | Transform and then Scale and Rotate. This opens up a small dialogue box in which values for both transformations can be specified. The corresponding dialogue box is shown in Figure 5.11.

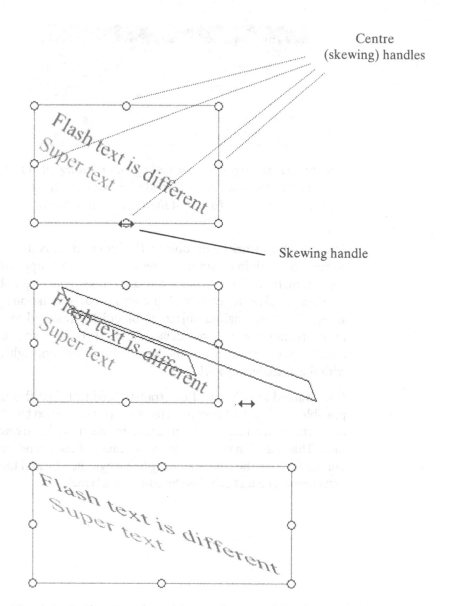

Centre
(skewing) handles

Skewing handle

Figure 5.10 *Skewing of an object makes use of the four centre handles,
which become available when the rotation option is selected.*

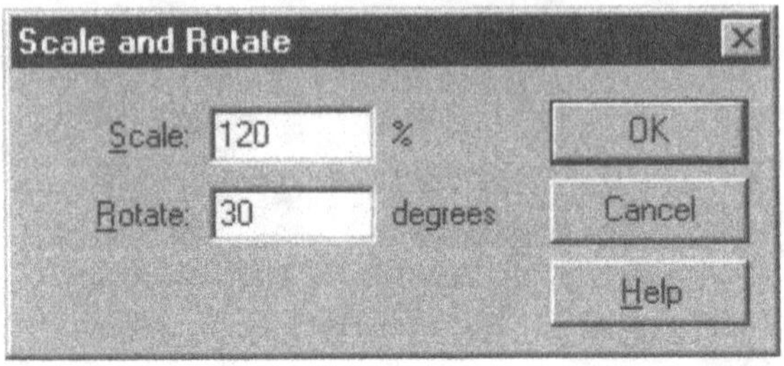

Figure 5.11 Dialogue box for scaling and rotating an object simultaneously. This is activated through selecting Modify | Transform *and then* Scale and Rotate.

The way Flash works with objects (including text) is that it stores the original status together with any applied transformations. So if a rotation is undertaken, the original coordinate values together with the amount of orientation is saved. This then enables objects to be quickly restored to a previous state. For this, we can use Modify | Transform and then Remove Transform or the Reset button (bottom right) with the Transform panel.

If we wanted to edit any of our transformed text then this is possible. As Figure 5.12 demonstrates, the respective text block is selected as with untransformed text (by means of the Arrow tool). This selection results in the appearance of the bounding box for the text, the corresponding line length handle and the text cursor. The text can then be edited as normal.

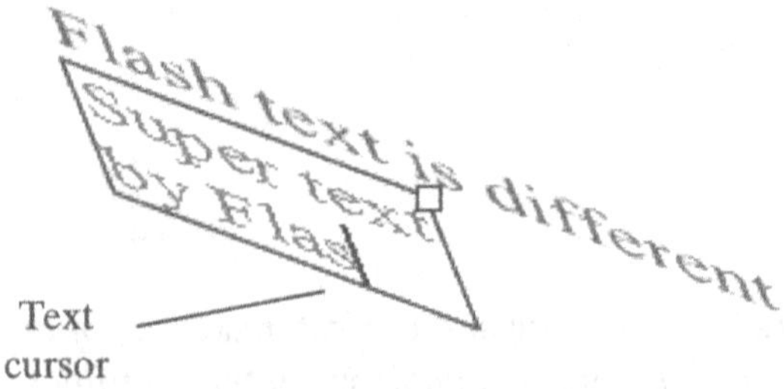

Text cursor

Figure 5.12 Transformed text (objects) can be edited by selecting the desired text block (via the Arrow tool). The text cursor appears within the transformed text and editing can take place as with normal text.

Editing text characters

In the previous section, we looked at some of the tools available for working with text blocks, conveniently referred to as text objects. Here we continue to focus on text, though we will concentrate more on individual words and characters rather than complete blocks of text. In other words, the tools that could be used to work with the text that is contained within the bounding box.

The immediate set of features that are applicable to characters and words can be found in the Character panel (see Figure 5.1). Apart from choosing an alternative font type and colour for selected characters or words within, say, a sentence, we have the option of specifying the height, spacing and position. The height is set by the corresponding slider, whilst the spacing is controlled by what Flash refers to as tracking. Here, uniform spacing can be inserted between characters through using the respective slider. The option of applying kerning to the selected characters or words is also available. The use of kerning is well established within the typographic industry where additional information is induced into the representation of a character so that pairs of characters are appropriately spaced. The kerning checkbox, on the Character panel, makes this available and is a useful feature for ensuring that text is aesthetically pleasing. In addition, we can position our selected text with reference to a baseline so that normal text is on this baseline, whilst superscript and subscript are above and below, respectively. An illustration of some of these features and the corresponding panel settings is shown in Figure 5.13.

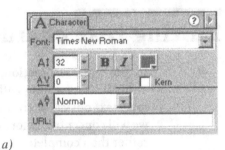

a)

b)

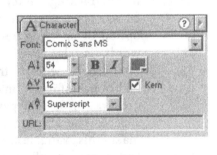

c)

Figure 5.13 *The application of character features to selected text (a, c, and t in the example shown) within a text block: (a) original, (b) change of font colour, height and tracking (character spacing), and (c) change of font type, use of kerning and with superscript position.*

Working with text shapes

So far, we have considered text as either a block or one consisting of a series of characters. There is another dimension that Flash allows when it comes to working with text. This is when text is not just seen in terms of characters, but as shapes. This is a powerful feature that enables individual characters to be treated similar to graphical objects. What this implies is that text can be coloured with a gradient or have its shape edited to yield a more artistic form. This opens up a whole new avenue for representing text that is more appealing in a movie.

In order to work with character shapes, we will first need to go through a conversion process. This takes the form of selecting a block of text (not individual characters) and using the option Modify | Break Apart. This will then allow us to work with the segments (for example, lines and curves representing the outlines and fills) of either individual characters or a group of characters. Effectively, the text is now a graphical object. As such, it can no longer be treated as text. So, text options such as font attributes and paragraph settings are no longer applicable. It is therefore important that the text reads correctly before breaking it into a graphical object. There is no option of converting it back to text mode. Figure 5.14 gives examples of working with text that has been converted to a graphical object.

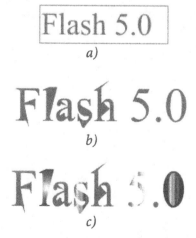

Figure 5.14 *Working with text shapes through using* Modify | Break Apart: *(a) original, (b) change of shape, and (c) use of fills including gradient fills.*

Chapter 6

Working with Imported Bitmaps

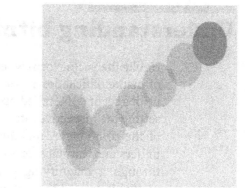

Introduction

Flash works with vectors to describe objects primarily to minimize the file size, for the necessary benefit of faster downloads and playback of movies. Working with vectors is fine, until there is a need to either generate or edit a bitmapped image. This could be in the form of a photograph that has been scanned, or we may have a library of bitmapped images that have been created using another graphical package. We would then want to include some of these images in our movie. The Flash environment allows for the usage of external images as bitmaps or for the conversion of these into vectors. When working with bitmaps, the size is controlled through a set of compression options that allow for optimized images.

In this chapter, we look at bitmaps and in particular the tools available in Flash that enable us to import, edit, convert, and work with such images.

Understanding bitmaps

Unlike the vector form where an object is defined by means of mathematical descriptions, in bitmaps an image is made up of a set of dots (called pixels). An image is formed through setting the respective intensity (for example, colour) for each of the components making up the image. The best way to understand bitmaps is to look at a printed photograph through a magnifying glass. This should show that the picture is created through using hundreds, if not thousands, of small dots. The colour of the dots will vary depending on the contents of the photograph. We can then say that the intensity of the dot (and, therefore, the pixel) correlates with the image at hand. It is interesting to note that the dots themselves are not visible to the naked eye when viewed from a distance since they blend into each other to form the picture.

When working with bitmaps, two attributes are important. One is the number of colours that each pixel will be able to represent. The more colours that are available to Flash, the more natural an image will look. The consequence of using more colours is that it will increase the movie size since more computer bits will be required to represent the increase in colour. Related to movie size, also, is the number of pixels that are used to display the image. This is referred to as the resolution and it governs the quality of the resulting image. Higher resolution leads to more pixels being used to store the picture. This in turn results in larger file sizes for the movie. The resolution of an image is measured in terms of the number of dots (pixels) per square inch (dpi).

In order to control the size of a movie, a compromise must be reached between the colour depth (number of bits per pixel being used to represent the colour), display resolution and the quality of the resulting image. Flash works with the original image and allows options to reduce its size by re-formatting the bitmap to either JPEG or GIF/PNG standards. These are compression techniques whose application is described later on in this chapter.

Importing bitmaps

Let us assume that we have created a bitmapped object and wish to include it in our Flash movie. How do we do this? There are two ways. The first is to use the import option on the Main menu. Here, we would choose File | Import. This will result in the respective dialogue box appearing. An example of this is shown in Figure 6.1. As you can see from this, there are a number of graphical formats that could be imported. Through selecting the appropriate file type and then the file, an image can be included in a Flash movie. Note that the image is imported as a self-contained unit so that it appears to float on the Stage. The effect shown in Figure 6.2 highlights another feature of the Flash environment whereby objects belonging to a single frame on the Stage can in fact be on different layers. This way, objects do not interfere with each other. This is a powerful feature which is discussed in detail in chapter 8.

The second approach to getting imported images into a Flash movie is through using the Clipboard. Here, we use the accepted approach of either cutting or copying an object within another package and then pasting it into Flash.

Although the way Flash treats the two approaches is slightly different, the effective result is the same, in that the bitmap appears on the Stage and can be included within a movie. In fact, a copy of the image (together with its description) is stored in the library. This means that the bitmapped image can be used again, as and when required. A detailed description of the library is given in the next chapter.

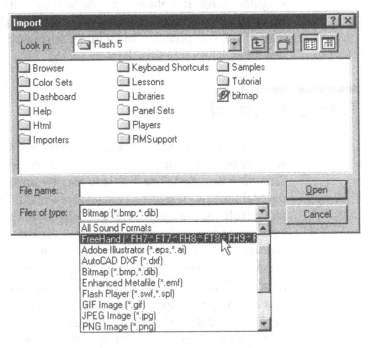

Figure 6.1 *The Import dialogue box.*

Editing bitmap images

The editing of any bitmaps is best undertaken by using a suitable package (such as Macromedia's Fireworks 3), which can usually be launched from within Flash. The Flash environment, however, supports a limited set of tools which allows for some editing of bitmaps.

One such feature is the ability to break apart a bitmap. This has the effect of separating the pixels in an image into discrete areas. This then allows for these to be selected (like vectored objects or its parts) and modified as desired through using some of the tools within the Toolbox. To break apart an image, we select it first and then choose Modify | Break Apart. Figure 6.3 illustrates the process for a bitmapped picture of a flower.

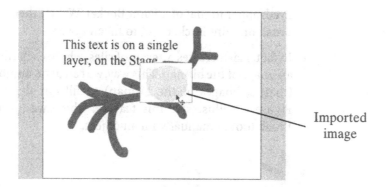

Figure 6.2 An imported bitmap, which floats on the existing artwork on the Stage.

We can use the bitmap as a fill for other objects. This is an attractive feature that allows us to fill an object with the contents of the bitmap. By content, we do not just mean colour or texture but the full contents of the bitmap. This is shown in Figure 6.4 where the Eyedropper tool (from the Toolbox) is used to capture the contents of the broken-up bitmapped image. This has the effect of the bitmap becoming the current fill and the active tool changing from the

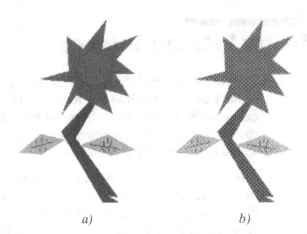

Figure 6.3 *The effect of breaking apart a bitmapped image, through selecting it and using* Modify | Break Apart: *(a) original image, and (b) after being split, where the image initially appears textured.*

Eyedropper to that of a Paint Bucket. We can then choose the Brush or Paint Bucket tool to fill an object.

In fact, Flash creates a series of tiles, where each tile contains an image of the bitmap. This way, we can use a number of tiles (that is, images of the bitmap) to fill our desired object. Figure 6.5 illustrates this feature, where we are using the Brush tool to manually fill an object.

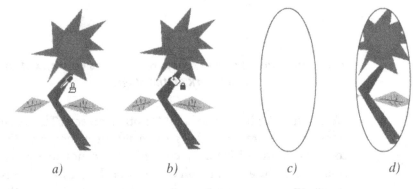

Figure 6.4 *Using a bitmap as a fill: (a) the Eyedropper tool being used to capture the broken-up bitmap, (b) once the bitmap has been captured, the tool changes automatically to that of a Paint Bucket, (c) the object (an ellipse) to be filled, and (d) the object after the bitmap fill.*

If we want to make changes to the bitmapped fill then this is possible. When, for example, the Paint Bucket tool is selected then within the Options section of the Toolbox is a button referred to as the Transform Fill modifier. This is shown in Figure 6.6. This modifier needs to be activated for changes to the bitmap fill to take place. Assuming this is the case, then we select the bitmap fill. Flash inserts a number of handles which allow for re-sizing, vertical and horizontal skewing, rotation and adjusting the centre of the bitmap. Figure 6.7 shows the positioning of these handles for a given bitmap fill. An illustration of these transformations is given in Figure 6.8, where it can be seen that the effect of these is applicable to all tiles. Note that these transformations are also applicable for gradient fills.

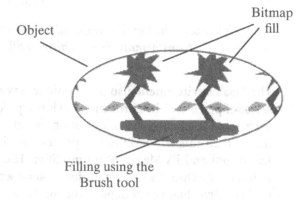

Figure 6.5 *Inserting tiles of the bitmap fill manually using the Brush tool.*

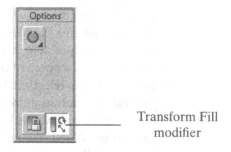

Figure 6.6 *The Transform Fill modifier is available within the Options section upon the Paint Bucket tool being activated.*

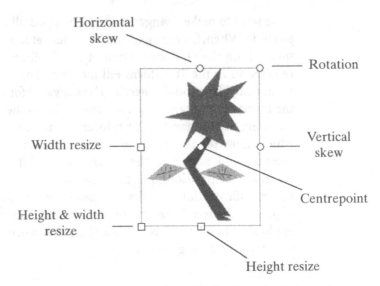

Figure 6.7 *The handles which allow the indicated transformations on a bitmap fill.*

The Flash environment also has a unique way of selecting a series of pixels within a broken-apart bitmap. For example, if we wanted to change the colour of an object representing a flower then this is possible. The process involves using the Lasso tool and its Magic Wand modifier. The latter can be found in the Options section of the Toolbox when the Lasso tool is active. Figure 6.9 depicts the location of the relevant modifiers.

The way the Magic Wand works is that it selects all pixels which have similar colours and are touching. What determines the correlation between pixel colours is the relevant settings for the Magic Wand. As Figure 6.10 shows there are two possible settings. The Threshold value determines the closeness in colour of two adjacent pixels to be included in the selection. Values can range from 1 to 200. Higher values result in more differing coloured pixels being selected, whilst a lower value will constrain the selection process to work with colours close to the original pixel. A value of 0 will require exact matching of colours to the original pixel. The Smoothing setting, on the other hand, refers to the form that the edges will take for the selected (part of the) bitmap. The available settings range from Pixels to Smooth. The former will leave the outline of the bitmap as defined by the pixels (in other words, one with no smoothing applied), whilst the latter uses techniques to smooth the edges out.

In general, to change the bitmap fill, we choose the Lasso tool and select the Magic Wand modifier. We then click the bitmap to select an area (or more than one area by clicking and adding to our selection). Next we choose a fill from the Colors section on the Toolbox and by using the Paint Bucket tool we apply the fill to the selected bitmap. The workings of this approach are animated in Figure 6.11.

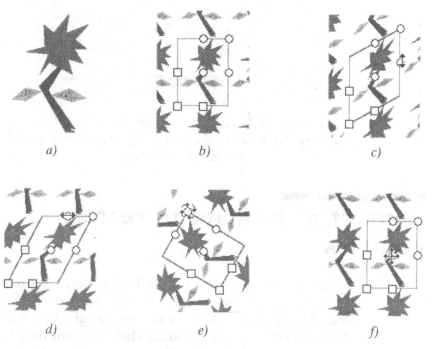

a)   *b)*   *c)*

d)   *e)*   *f)*

Figure 6.8 *The various transformations which are possible for a bitmap fill: (a) original, (b) scaling of width and height, (c) vertical skewing, (d) horizontal skewing, (e) rotation, and (f) re-positioning of centre.*

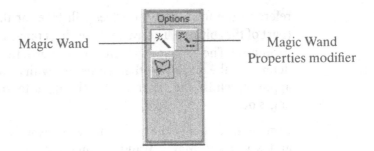

Magic Wand ——————— Magic Wand
                                          Properties modifier

*Figure 6.9 The Magic Wand modifiers can be found within
the Options section of the Toolbox when the Lasso tool is
selected.*

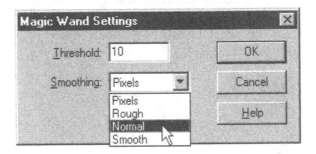

*Figure 6.10 The dialogue box for setting the colour
matching threshold and the level of edge smoothing required
for the selected bitmap.*

Converting bitmaps to vector graphics

As mentioned earlier, bitmaps can lead to large file sizes,
distortion can take place when they are transformed (for
example, rotation can lead to objects having rough edges), and
the number of tools available within Flash for editing them is
rather constrained. Therefore Flash offers the Trace Bitmap
feature to convert bitmaps into vector graphics and thus
provide an alternative to working with bitmapped images. The
vector representation is formed through identifying areas that

have common attributes (for example, colour) and realizing their outlines by using line and curve segments, as required.

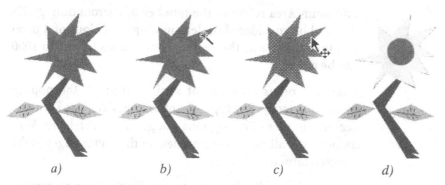

a)   b)   c)   d)

Figure 6.11 The use of the Magic Wand modifier to change the contents (for example, colour) of selected parts of a bitmap fill: (a) original, (b) Magic Wand being positioned for selection, (c) selection of connecting and similar pixels through a single click, and (d) changing colour for the selection.

To produce a vector representation, select the (unbroken) bitmapped image and then choose Modify | Trace Bitmap. This results in the dialogue box shown in Figure 6.12. There are four parameters associated with this option that allow us to control how closely the resulting vector graphic matches with the given bitmap. The parameters are:

- Color Threshold
- Minimum Area
- Curve Fit
- Corner Threshold.

The Color Threshold determines the colour correlation of two pixels that are touching. This is achieved by comparing the respective colours and seeing if the difference in the RGB (red, green and blue) values is less than the Color Threshold. If this is the case then the two pixels are considered to have the same colour. Higher values for the Color Threshold result in fewer colours appearing in the vector form. This, however, results in larger areas being specified and fewer vector segments are used. So, a balance needs to be kept between image quality and the file size for the vectored form. The range for the Color Threshold is from 1 to 500.

Minimum Area refers to the number of surrounding pixels that will be considered in determining the colour of a pixel and thus the size of the vector shape. Values from 1 to 1000 can be entered.

Curve Fit offers an array of settings through the pop-up menu to specify the type of smoothness required for the vector outlines. The options range from Pixels to Very Smooth and allow for the closeness of the vector edges to the selected bitmap.

Corner Threshold allows us to specify the type of corners that should be used for the vector version. The range is Many Corners to Few Corners. If Many Corners is selected then this will give sharp corners that reflect the bitmapped image more closely. Few Corners will yield smoother, more rounded, corners.

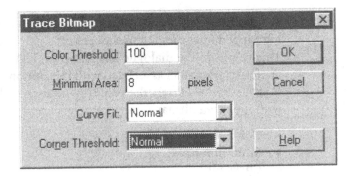

Figure 6.12 Dialogue box for the Trace Bitmap command, used to convert a bitmap into a corresponding vector form.

The outcome from the Trace Bitmap command will depend on both the settings used and the contents of the bitmap image. Figure 6.13 gives an illustrative example of this. Working with photographs, for instance, requires that the vector version resembles closely the bitmap form. So, typical settings for this (as recommended by Macromedia) are 10 for Color Threshold, 1 pixel for Minimum Area, Pixels for

Curve Fit and Many Corners for Corner Threshold. The consequence of doing this is, however, large file sizes and, in fact, if in general the original bitmap contains complex shapes and many colours, the resulting vector form can return a larger file size than the given bitmap.

The file size (together with other attributes) of the objects on the Stage can be viewed through using the Bandwidth Profiler feature. This is activated by choosing Control | Test Scene or Control | Test Movie, which in turn opens the Output window. We then choose View | Bandwidth Profiler. The resulting window is shown in Figure 6.14 for the case where only the object shown in Figure 6.13 is placed on the Stage. This way, the size of the bitmap can be compared with its vector equivalence. In essence, some experimentation needs to take place before deciding on the best values for the Trace Bitmap parameters.

Setting bitmap properties

Within the Flash environment is a dialogue box which provides information about the selected bitmap and also the options of smoothing and compression. This is opened through choosing Window | Library. Select the desired object from the list and then click the right mouse button. As Figure 6.15 shows, we then choose Properties from the context menu. This opens the Bitmap Properties dialogue box shown in Figure 6.16. We see that this gives the name (including path and date of creation), resolution (including colour depth) and a preview of the bitmap. The name can be changed, whilst the preview gives the most up-to-date version including any changes that may have taken place within the dialogue box. The Update button is used to link and reflect any changes made by a graphics-editing program to the bitmap in the preview window. The Test button is used to refresh the bitmap preview with any new settings within the dialogue box. We can also select an area within the bitmap to preview by clicking and dragging to specify the desired region. This is depicted in Figure 6.17.

If we wish to anti-alias (introduce levels of grey or shades of colour to) the edges of the bitmap, then the Allow Smoothing option needs to be checked. In addition, we have two choices of compressing the bitmap (through the Compression options). Both choices determine the type of compression that will be employed in the creation of a Flash movie. The Photo (JPEG) option compresses the bitmap image into JPEG format. We can then check the Use document default quality option to maintain the original compression quality associated with the imported bitmap. Otherwise, we can leave this box unchecked and enter a value between 1 to 100 in the Quality text box. The higher the value, the better the quality, but at the cost of lower compression. In other words, the reduction in file size will be minimal if we want the compressed form to maintain most, if not all, of the original bitmap contents. Through using the Test button, we can gauge the impact of using different quality values on the bitmap image. Furthermore, a text window appears at the bottom of the dialogue box indicating the effect of the quality value on the file size (in bytes and as a percentage). This is shown in Figure 6.18.

The second type of compression that is available is Lossless (PNG/GIF). This is ideally suited for non-photographic images which make use of simple shapes and more importantly have relatively small colour content. As the name suggests, the attraction of this form is that it works by removing any redundancies within the bitmap and the actual content is not compromised. In other words, the compressed form reflects the original. Again, the Test button can be used to view the effect of this for a given bitmap.

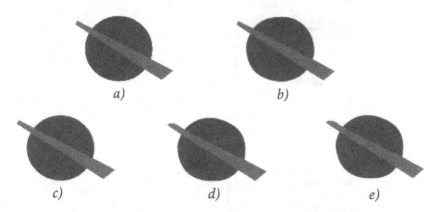

a)   *b)*

c)   *d)*   *e)*

Figure 6.13 *The effect of using different settings for the Trace Bitmap: (a) original bitmap, (b) settings of Color Threshold = 100, Maximum Area = 8, Curve Fit = Normal, Corner Threshold = Normal; (c) settings of Color Threshold = 100, Maximum Area = 1,Curve Fit = Pixels, Corner Threshold = Many Corners; (d) settings of Color Threshold = 100, Maximum Area = 1, Curve Fit = Very Smooth, Corner Threshold = Few Corners; and (e) settings of Color Threshold = 100, Maximum Area = 20, Curve Fit = Very Smooth, Corner Threshold = Few Corners.*

In case we need to work with another bitmap within the dialogue box, then there is a button labelled Import which allows for a new image to be opened. The effect of this would be to substitute the current image being referenced and displayed on the preview window with the one that is to be imported.

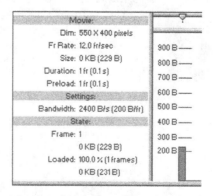

Figure 6.14 *The Bandwidth Profiler, showing (apart from other attributes) the size of the file (in this case after the conversion from bitmap to vector).*

Figure 6.15 Launching the Bitmap
Properties dialogue box.

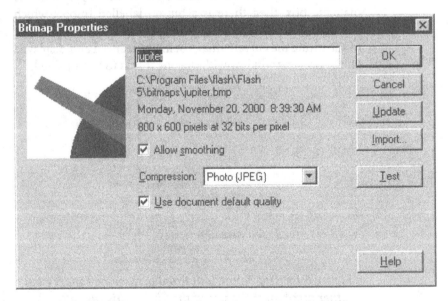

Figure 6.16 The Bitmap Properties dialogue box.

Figure 6.17 *Within the preview window, different parts of an object can be viewed through clicking and dragging, as desired.*

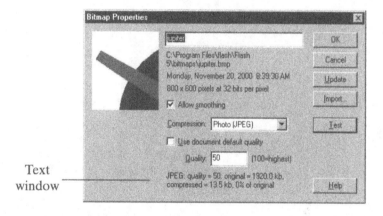

Text
window

Figure 6.18 *The effect of using the Test button after a quality value has been entered is that the preview window is updated and a text window appears showing the impact of the settings on the file size.*

Chapter 7

Using the Library, Symbols and Instances

Introduction

We have looked at the Flash environment, thus far, in terms of using its various features and tools to create or edit static graphical images. We have seen that, even working with these tools, the environment provides a natural, but unique way of developing our desired movie. Our main goal would be to produce an animation of some kind that meets a particular need. For this, we would require to re-use some objects again and again. Maybe the colour or shape would change in different scenes, but the underlying object would be the same as was probably created and used in scene 1. Even if we do not want to, or do not need to, re-use a graphical image, it would still make sense to have a list of these available, where the properties of each image can be view and modified, if required.

As you may expect, Flash supports the idea of having a library which stores information about objects that appear within a movie. The Library is rather comprehensive in that it stores bitmap and vector images (that is, both imported and those created in Flash), text, sounds, animation and buttons. In fact, just about every object that is used within a movie and appears on the screen has its details registered within the Library.

In the world of Flash, the term 'symbol' is used to denote a graphical object in the library (others are simply referred to as their respective names, for example sounds are called sounds). The use of an object on the Stage is referred to as an instance. So, we can have one symbol, with several instances of it appearing within a movie.

In this chapter we look at the Library, its interface and what it has to offer, together with introducing and understanding the use of symbols and their instances.

The Library interface

As an object is created or imported onto the Stage, a copy (symbol) is placed in the Library, together with its attributes.

This includes information about its frequency of usage within a movie, the nature of the symbol and when it was last modified, as well as a host of other information. As a file management system it allows for creating shortcuts, renaming objects and fast deletion. In addition, the environment automatically opens the Library window at the start of a session, if it was opened in the previous session. The contents of the Library can be viewed, edited and used as desired. We can open the Library window either through selecting `Window | Library` or by clicking the Library button on the Launcher bar at the bottom of the application (Stage) window. The latter is shown in Figure 7.1. There is also a third way of opening the Library window. This is where the current movie needs to make use of symbols belonging to another movie. This is looked at later in this chapter.

Library
button

Figure 7.1 Use of the Launcher bar to open the Library window.

The resulting Library window is depicted in Figure 7.2. Although the window looks innocent in that there is a preview section, a list of symbols and some buttons, what it actually offers is a sophisticated management system for organizing symbols.

Let us start by looking at the Wide State and Narrow State. These refer to the size of the actual window and in particular the width of the window. The purpose of these is to switch between providing basic information (for example, the name of a symbol) to that of having more columns appearing that provide additional information about the symbols. The effect of these two buttons is illustrated in Figure 7.3. The buttons yield a fast way of resizing the window, though we could always use the accepted way of click and drag to undertake the same.

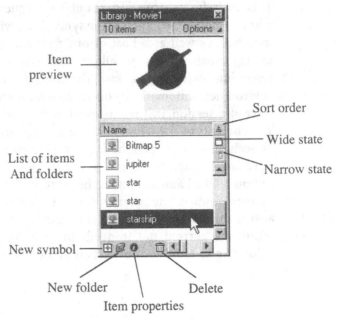

Figure 7.2 *The Library window.*

We can sort the entries in the Library by a particular column. As Figure 7.4 illustrates, this is achieved through selecting the column header. The order is sorted alphanumerically with

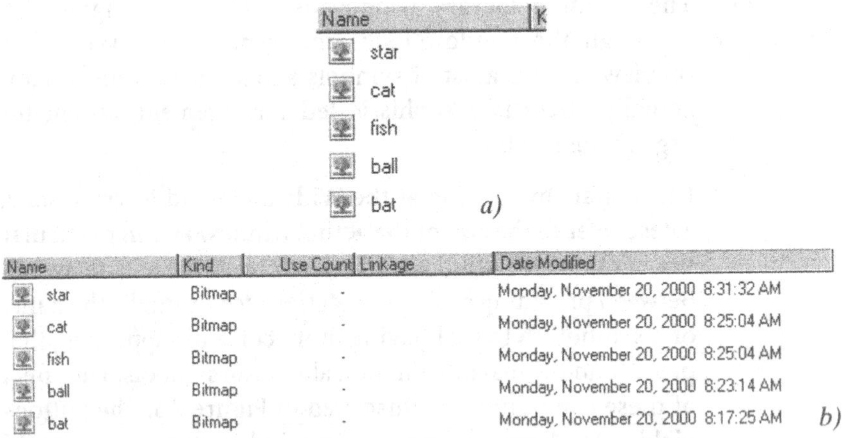

Figure 7.3 *Resizing the Library window through using the respective buttons: (a) Narrow State, and (b) Wide State.*

reference to the contents of the selected column. The Sort Order button can be used to toggle between ascending and descending alphanumeric sequence.

Name	Kind	Use Count	Linkage	Date Modified
ball	Bitmap	·		Monday, November 20, 2000 8:23:14 AM
bat	Bitmap	·		Monday, November 20, 2000 8:17:25 AM
cat	Bitmap	·		Monday, November 20, 2000 8:25:04 AM
fish	Bitmap	·		Monday, November 20, 2000 8:25:04 AM

a)

Name	Kind	Use Count	Linkage	Date Modified
jupiter	Bitmap	·		Monday, November 20, 2000 8:39:30 AM
star	Bitmap	·		Monday, November 20, 2000 8:31:32 AM
star	Bitmap	·		Monday, November 20, 2000 8:31:32 AM
cat	Bitmap	·		Monday, November 20, 2000 8:25:04 AM

b)

Figure 7.4 *Sort symbols through selecting the header of the reference column: (a) Name column, and (b) Date column.*

Renaming an item can be done in several ways:

- Double-click the name of the symbol and enter the new name in the text field, or
- Right-click the item and then choose Rename, or
- Select the item and click Symbol Properties button, and Name in the resulting dialogue box, or
- Select the item and choose Rename from the Options menu.

Note that this changes the name of the symbol, but it does not affect the name of an imported file.

The Delete button can be used to remove a selected symbol from the Library. Before removing an item, we should note whether it is being used within a movie. This information is contained within the Use Count column. Deleting an item from the Library also removes it from all instances or occurrences within a movie. There is no Restore option, so care must be taken when deleting items from the Library.

Working with Library folders

Flash supports the creation of folders in the same way we would use Windows Explorer to set up a hierarchical structure to store files. The folders provide an efficient way of organizing symbols in a meaningful way. This may not seem important at the beginning of a production, but as more and more objects are placed on the Stage, the use of folders becomes essential. Apart from locating symbols quickly, the folders can also help in avoiding duplication whereby the type of symbol within the Library can be compared with what is required. Combined with the Sort Order (using the desired column as a reference) option, symbols can be organized effectively.

We can create a new folder either by clicking the New Folder button at the bottom of the Library window (see Figure 7.2) or using the Options menu (available on the top right of the Library window). As Figure 7.5 shows, in the latter case, we would then select New Folder from the pop-up menu. Sub-folders can be created in the same manner. In this case, we would need to have selected an item within the folder where we wish to include a sub-folder. Having done this, we can choose either of the two approaches mentioned above to create a sub-folder.

A symbol when created is placed in the selected folder. If no folder is selected then it is placed at the root folder of the Library. A symbol can be moved to a chosen folder by clicking it and dragging it to the desired folder.

We can also place a selected item in a new folder. The way this is undertaken is by selecting the item and then using the Library Options (pop-up) menu to create a new folder. When this is done, a dialogue box appears requesting a name for the new folder. By naming the new folder and clicking OK, the selected item is automatically moved into the newly created folder.

Opening and closing a folder can be accomplished by:

- Double clicking the desired folder, or
- By using the Library Options (pop-up) menu. In this case, we would choose Expand Folder to open it or Collapse Folder to close it.

If we wanted to open or close all folders then this is possible. We would choose respectively from the Library Options menu Expand All Folders or Collapse All Folders.

To remove a folder from the Library, we will first select the desired folder and then use the Delete button (see Figure 7.2). Alternatively, we can choose Delete from the Library Options menu to remove a selected folder. As in the case of deleting an item, Flash displays a warning message. This is shown in Figure 7.6. This acts as a reminder that the delete operation will remove the folder together with any items that it contains. It will also remove instances of items appearing on the Stage. Once these are removed, they cannot be restored.

Figure 7.5 *Using the Library Options pop-up menu to create a new folder.*

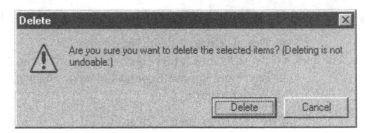

Figure 7.6 Warning message that appears when deleting an item or folder from the Library.

Working with imported files

In addition to symbols, the Library can also contain imported files. These could be in the form of video clips, sound tracks or bitmaps. These files would have been created and edited using an appropriate software package, which in turn produces a version suitable for the production being authored in Flash. The files themselves are listed like other symbols, though their respective icons reflect their type. Imported files in the Library are treated similarly to other items, except that there are two additional options that become available. The first one allows for attributes associated with the imported file to be viewed and changed. The second option simply allows for updates of the imported file to be recognized.

We view the attributes of an imported item either by clicking the Properties button (on the bottom of the Library window, see Figure 7.2) or through the Library Options menu and then choosing Properties. This opens a dialogue box which shows the attributes for the selected imported file. Figure 7.7 gives an illustrative example for a sound file.

Any changes made by an external editor to a file that has already been imported into Flash can be recognized without going through the process of importing again. Flash allows for this through the Update selection, available within the Library Options menu. Therefore, to use the latest version of an imported file, we select it and then choose Update.

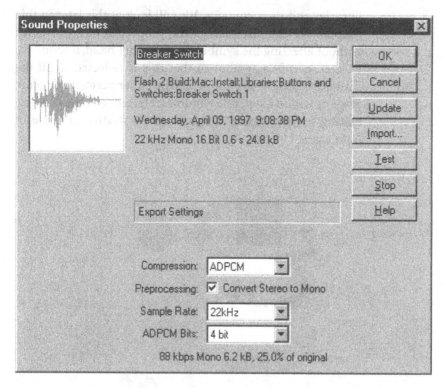

Figure 7.7 *Properties Dialogue box for an imported item stored in the Library.*

Creating symbols

The creation and use of symbols is an important process within Flash as it dictates to a large extent the file size of the resulting movie. File size is kept to a minimum as only the symbol is stored and not its instances. In fact, instances are also stored but not completely since they are referenced to the symbol in question. Another advantage is that the playback speed for the movie would be enhanced since a symbol will be downloaded to a browser only once. In addition, the symbols facilitate reusability where they can be employed again and again within a movie. Moreover, symbols can be reused by other movies through sharing libraries and their contents. We will look at this later in this chapter. We can also change the properties of an instance without affecting the symbol. On the other hand, if required, we can modify a symbol so that this is reflected in all the instances. Editing of symbols can be either performed on the Stage or within a separate window (referred to as the symbol-editing mode). Figure 7.8 gives an illustrative example of both cases.

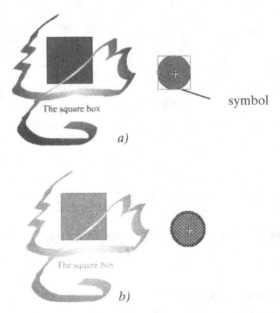

symbol

a)

b)

Figure 7.8 Editing a symbol: (a)on the Stage, with a bounding box , or (b) using a separate window, where the rest of the objects have been dimmed.

Flash works with three types of symbols: Graphics, Buttons and Movie clips. In this section, we will focus on symbols that are graphical in nature. The other two, especially Button, types are looked at in later chapters. We can choose to convert existing objects into symbols or create an empty symbol and then decide on the object it will represent. To create a new symbol for selected objects, we choose `Insert | Convert to Symbol`. This opens the Properties dialogue box for the symbols, an example of which is shown in Figure 7.9. We can then choose the name and behaviour type (that is, whether the symbol is a graphic, button or a movie clip). By pressing OK, the symbol is added to the Library and the selection on the Stage becomes an instance of the symbol.

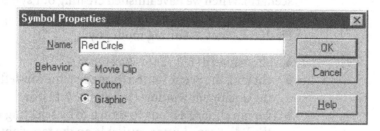

Figure 7.9 *Properties dialogue box for symbols.*

In order to edit the symbol, we will need to use the symbol-editing mode. This is reflected in the way Flash shows the selection of the instance on the Stage. Figure 7.10 depicts the scenario where the object, before becoming a symbol, turns textured when selected and the use of a bounding box when it becomes a symbol.

As mentioned earlier, we can also create an empty symbol. Assuming that no objects are selected on the Stage, then this can be done by any of the three approaches listed below:

- by choosing `Insert | New Symbol`, or
- through clicking the New Symbol button located at the bottom-left corner of the Library window (see Figure 7.2), or
- by selecting New Symbol in the Library Options menu.

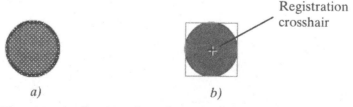

Figure 7.10 *Selection of an object: (a) before being converted to a symbol, and (b) the use of a bounding box to indicate that it has become a symbol and we will need to use symbol-editing mode to make changes to it.*

This then opens the Symbols Properties dialogue box. As before, we specify the name and behaviour type and press OK. The effect this time, however, is that Flash opens the symbol-editing mode in anticipation that we want to either create or import a symbol. Figure 7.11 illustrates this scenario. When we have finished creating our symbol, we can then return to our current scene (that is, the Stage or what Flash calls movie-editing mode) by:

- choosing `Edit | Edit Movie`, or
- clicking the Scene button located on the top-left corner of the document window (see Figure 7.11), or
- we can choose a scene to return to by selecting it through the Edit Scene button available on the top-right corner of the document window. This is shown in Figure 7.12.

The newly created symbol is added to the Library and can be added to a scene, as and when required.

Often there is a need to create a new symbol which either differs slightly from an existing symbol, or the new symbol needs to be created with reference to one that has already appears within a scene. Flash provides two options within the Library window for doing this. By selecting a desired symbol, we can either:

- right click and choose Duplicate from the context menu, or
- select Duplicate from the Library Options menu.

Current scene   Symbol name   Edit scene   Edit symbol

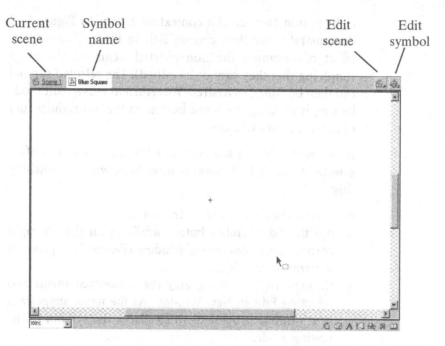

Figure 7.11 *Symbol-editing mode for the case where a new symbol (blue square) has been created.*

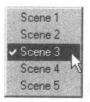

Figure 7.12 *Pop-up menu for Edit scene button showing available scenes, which can be used to return from symbol-editing mode to movie-editing mode.*

Editing symbols

As mentioned earlier, symbols can be edited on the Stage or via symbol-editing mode, which uses a separate window. To edit a symbol on the Stage, we simply select it and click the right button to open the contextual menu. As Figure 7.13 demonstrates, we then choose Edit in Place. This has the effect of dimming the non-selected items on the Stage (implying that they cannot be edited). The selected symbol can then be edited as desired. We return to movie-edit mode by simply clicking the Scene button on the top-right corner of the document window.

If we wanted to use the symbol-editing mode to modify a selected symbol, then there are three basic ways of launching this:

- we can choose Modify | Instance, or
- use the Edit Symbol button available on the top-right corner of the document window (Figure 7.14 gives an illustration of this), or
- through right clicking and the contextual menu and selecting Edit in New Window. As the name suggests, a new window is opened which places the symbol in the editing mode.

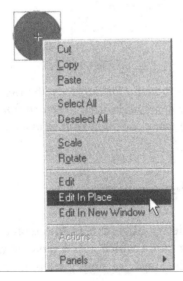

Figure 7.13 Selecting to edit a symbol on the Stage.

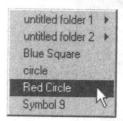

*Figure 7.14 Pop-up menu for the Symbol List button;
selection of a symbol will activate the symbol-editing mode.*

Creating and editing instances

Having generated symbols, we can then make use of them by employing their instances within a scene. The instance acts as an index to the symbol in the Library. The full description is always with the symbol, though changes to instances can be made without affecting the respective symbol. We can create an instance of a symbol by using the Library and dragging the required instance onto the Stage. Figure 7.15 gives an animated illustration of this process.

Once we have an instance of a symbol on the Stage, we can change its attributes without affecting the symbol properties. To do this, we make use of the Instance panel. This can be opened either from the Launcher bar (bottom-right corner of the document window, see Figure 7.16) or by Window | Panels and then Instance. The resulting panel is shown in Figure 7.17. Once we have the Instance panel opened, we can move directly to symbol-editing mode by clicking the Edit Symbol button shown in Figure 7.17.

In addition, we can make use of the Effect panel to assist us in the editing process. Choose Window | Panels and then Effects. This opens the panel shown in Figure 7.18.

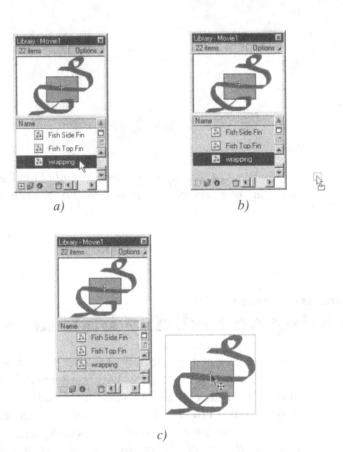

Figure 7.15 *Creation of an instance for a chosen symbol: (a) selection from Library; (b) positioning of the symbol on the Stage. The cursor indicates the location of the registration crosshair; and (c) an instance of the symbol on the Stage.*

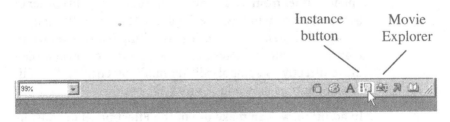

Figure 7.16 *Opening the Instance panel by using the Launcher bar.*

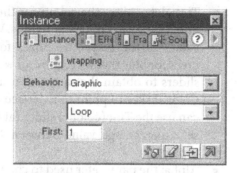

Figure 7.17 The Instance panel.

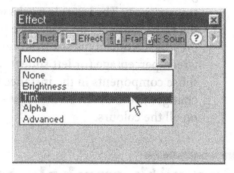

Figure 7.18 The Effects panel.

We can see that there are a number of tools available to modify an instance. These allow for specifying colour effects, assigning actions, setting the graphics mode and changing the behaviour. This way, an instance can possess properties that are different from the originating symbol. For example, if we wanted to change the colour and transparency of an instance, we will select the instance and then launch the Effect panel. As Figure 7.18 shows, there are four parameters which can be adjusted. With reference to Figure 7.19, the way these work is as follows:

● Brightness: controls the level of intensity with a range of –100% (black) to 100% (white). We can either enter a value in the text box or use the slider. The effect of any change is applied on the fly so that we can view it on the Stage.

- Tint: determines the colour for the instance. There are a number of ways of changing this. We can choose to enter values in the respective boxes for the amount of red, green, or blue that we require, or we can use the respective sliders to obtain the same. Alternatively, we can use the Color Picker to point to a desired colour. In addition we can use the Tint (colour) slider (at the top of the panel) to set a percentage value between 1 (transparent) to 100 (opaque).
- Alpha: the parameter used to change the transparency of the instance.
- Advanced: provides settings to separately adjust the red, green, and blue colours, together with values for the transparency. The left side works with percentages, whilst the right with actual values. The percentage values affect only the colour in question. For example, a change in the Green percentage (or left slider) will be reflected in only those components in the instance that are green. Making changes to the Green on the right side will have an impact on all the colours.

Working with symbols and instances

There are a number of additional features that make it convenient to work with symbols and instances. For example, we can assign a different symbol to an instance. This has the effect of changing the instance to mirror the new symbol, but the instance maintains any modifications (such as rotation, scaling, etc.) that may have been applied to it. The instance of the new symbol also appears on the Stage at the same location as before.

We assign a different symbol to an instance by using the Instance panel. Select the instance first and then Window | Panels and choose Instance. As Figure 7.20 shows there is a Swap Symbol button at the bottom-right corner of the resulting panel. We click this to get the corresponding dialogue box shown in Figure 7.21. From this, the desired new (replacement) symbol is chosen for the selected instance.

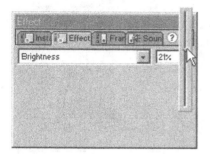

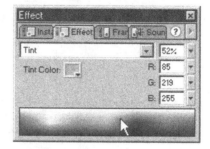

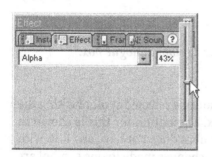

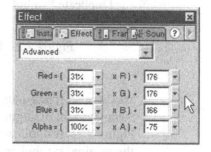

Figure 7.19 *Dialogue boxes for the four parameters which can be adjusted within the Effect panel.*

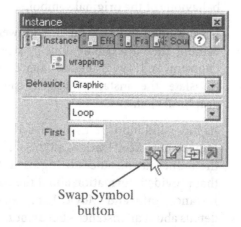

Swap Symbol button

Figure 7.20 *Instance panel showing the Swap Symbol button.*

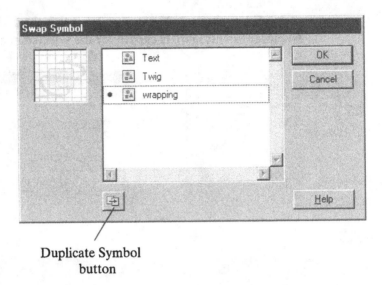

Duplicate Symbol
button

Figure 7.21 *Swap Symbol dialogue box.*

We can also create a duplicate of a selected symbol within the Swap Symbol dialogue box. The button for this is shown in Figure 7.21. A duplicate symbol does not have any link with the original symbol, in that changes made to one symbol are not transferred to the other. We may then change the behaviour of the duplicate (via the Instance panel), for example, to meet a desired design goal without affecting the behaviour of the original symbol.

If we wanted to break the link between an instance and its symbol, then this can be done by selecting the instance and choosing Modify | Break Apart. The effect of this is to translate the instance into a collection of ungrouped graphical elements.

As more and more items are placed on the Stage, it becomes important to keep track of all the symbols and, in particular, the numerous instances being used. Flash has three panels that provide information about the current state of a movie: Instance, Info and Movie Explorer. The first panel gives details about an instance's behaviour. The second returns the coordinate (size and position) of an instance. The Movie

Explorer panel is rather comprehensive and is shown in Figure 7.22. This lists the contents of the current movie, including instances, symbols and any associated actions. It can be opened via Window | Movie Explorer or through the button on the Launcher bar (see Figure 7.16). The main purpose of the Movie Explorer is to facilitate flexibility in viewing, modifying and organizing the contents of a movie.

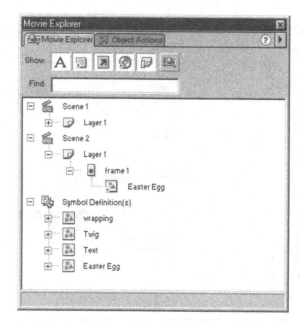

Figure 7.22 The Movie Explorer panel.

Working with shared symbols

As a movie is being produced, a number of items are created either within Flash or via an external package and stored in the Library. Once in the Library, they can be used again and again, as and when required, to make a desired production. We may want to use a particular set of symbols or a Library for another movie. To make this possible, Flash allows us to create what is referred to as Common Libraries. The easiest way of doing this is first to develop a Flash movie with an appropriate Library. Then in order to use this Library in another movie, we choose `File | Open As Library`. This adds the Library to the common set of libraries available to other movies. We can choose `Window | Common Libraries` to get access to all the available Libraries and their contents. Figure 7.23 gives an illustrative example.

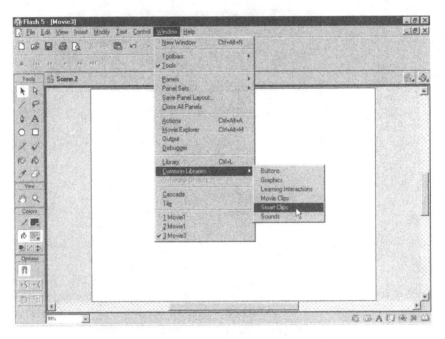

Figure 7.23 Activating Common Libraries menu.

It should also be noted that Flash comes with a set of built-in Libraries (such as Buttons, Graphics, Movie Clips, and Sounds). These are also shown in Figure 7.23. We can add to this list and have our symbols permanently available for other movies. The way to do this is to first to realize that the Library menu reflects what is currently stored on the hard disk drive within the Libraries folder. By placing a Flash movie in this folder, we make the library (and not the movie) available for other productions.

Chapter 8

Understanding Layers

Introduction

When we start to work on a Flash movie, we begin by creating symbols that are to be included in the production. Instances of these are then placed on the Stage as and when required. To date, we have worked with the Stage as a single bed where all instances reside. This is true in the sense that instances are organized and placed on the Stage, but the Stage itself consists of several layers. A layer is like a transparent sheet, where each layer has its own set of objects.

The Stage comprises a number of layers that are stacked together to form a scene. They normally work independently of each other so that objects placed on a layer can be edited without affecting objects on another layer. Using more layers does not increase the file size of the resulting Flash movie. We can use as many layers as necessary. They can be used to create separate animations for the same scene, or parts of the same animation can use a number of layers. A layer could be used to hold the background to a scene, whilst other layers are used to generate the animation. It is often advantageous to use different layers for different types of objects.

In this chapter, we look at the use of layers and, in particular, the numerous benefits that they offer.

Creating layers

Flash provides a range of buttons that allow us to work with layers. Through these, we can create, delete, name, hide, lock, show outline and mask layers. There is a set of layers which assist in the creation of an animation. The Flash environment allows for easy access and viewing of these through a layer interface which is attached to the Timeline. This is shown in Figure 8.1.

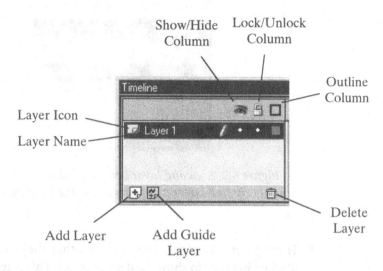

Figure 8.1 *The layer interface, which is attached to the Timeline.*

We can choose how to use these layers. Different objects, for example, can be placed on different layers. When we begin our Flash movie, there is usually only one layer (which has the default name Layer 1). As we start to develop our movie, we would want to use more layers to better organize the production. We can do this by first choosing to create more layers by any of the following ways:

- Use the Add Layer button (see Figure 8.1), or
- Choose Insert | Layer, or
- Through right-clicking on a layer name in the interface and then choosing Insert Layer from the context menu.

The new layer appears as a new row on the Timeline, which in turn is above the current selected layer on the interface. This is shown in Figure 8.2, where the new layer (Layer 2) is shown highlighted and becomes the active layer. An active layer has a pencil icon attached to it. Note that only one layer can be active at any moment in time, though (as we will see in the next section) we can select more than one layer.

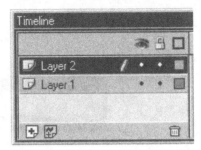

Figure 8.2 *A second layer being added to a movie. The newly created Layer 2 appears above the existing Layer 1.*

Having two (or more) layers means that they need to be stacked in order to show the desired effect. This is referred to as the stacking order and it determines the sequencing of layers. Objects on the top layer appear in front of objects on the next layer. This way, we are able to add depth to our movie. Figure 8.3 gives an animated illustration of this, where we note that the stacking order starts with the top layer. This is always the first layer shown on the layer interface.

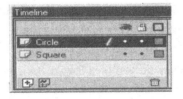

Figure 8.3 *Illustration of how the order of layers affects the appearance of objects on the Stage.*

Editing layers

Just like objects on a Stage, to manipulate layers we will need to select them. As Figure 8.4 shows, we can select a layer by doing one of the following:

- Clicking the respective layer's name in the layer interface, or
- Clicking a frame on the Timeline which appears in the same row as the respective layer, or
- Selecting an object belonging to the layer.

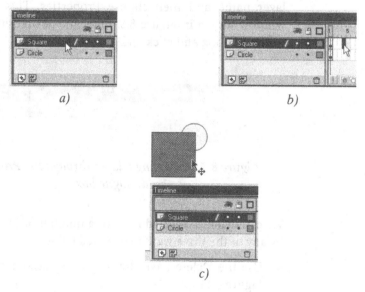

a)

b)

c)

Figure 8.4 *Selection of a layer can be performed either through: (a) the layer interface, or (b) via a frame on the Timeline, or (c) through an object appearing on the respective layer.*

We can also select more than one layer at a time by Shift-clicking the names of the layers on the layer interface. This will select a block of continuous layers, for example, layers 3 to 7. If we wanted to select another layer not belonging to this group (say, layer 10) then we would use Control-click (instead of Shift-click).

One of the first editing tasks that we will need to do is to rename the layers so that the names have more meaning to our work. We do not need to change names as the Flash environment automatically gives names to layers (such as Layer 5, Layer 6, and so on) but after a while it becomes difficult to remember what these layers are actually referring to. It is therefore much better to give names which reflect the layer's contents. The easiest way of doing this is through double-clicking the layer name on the layer interface and entering the desired name. We can also use the context menu to do the same. In this case, we would need to right-click the layer name and then choose Properties. This opens the window shown in Figure 8.5. Enter the desired name in the Name text box and click OK.

Figure 8.5 Renaming a layer through the Properties dialogue box.

We can delete a selected layer or a number of selected layers by any of the three ways mentioned below:

- Use the Delete Layer button in the layer interface (see Figure 8.1), or
- Drag the selected layer to the Delete Layer button, or
- Through the Delete Layer option which becomes available through the context menu after right-clicking the layer name.

When a layer is deleted, clearly all items associated with it are all also removed from the Stage. Although this appears to be rather a defeatist option, in fact it is exactly the opposite. If, for example, our movie was organized in terms of layers for each type of item appearing in a scene, we may well decide to change the background or the music track. This may be near the end of the development phase, when the movie contains hundreds, if not thousands, of objects. Having organized our movie in terms of layers, we can easily select the layers in question, delete them and create new layers with the appropriate contents. Moreover, if we unintentionally delete a layer, we can restore it through the Undo button.

Sometimes it becomes necessary to use a new layer to build on an existing layer. In this case, we may want to use all or part of the contents of the existing layer. Flash caters for both scenarios. To copy a layer (and therefore its complete contents), we first create a new layer using, say, the Add Layer button on the layer interface. We then select the layer whose contents we want to copy and choose Edit | Copy Frames. By clicking the new layer and selecting Edit | Paste Frames, the contents are copied. Note that we will get the same options (to copy and paste) using the context menu associated with the layers.

We can also copy blocks of layers. Again, we create a new layer where we want the contents to be copied. This acts as the first layer for the paste phase. Flash automatically creates additional layers with respect to the block of layers selected. We then select a block of layers and use the same options as for copying and pasting a single layer. As Figure 8.6 illustrates, this returns an exact copy of the originals. Both the names and the layers' relative positions are maintained.

If we wanted to copy objects across layers (rather than the complete contents of layers) then this can be accomplished by selecting the desired objects and then using the copy and paste commands. As Figure 8.7 shows, however, there are two ways of pasting the objects: Paste and Paste in Place. The difference between the two is the placement of the objects on the new layer. The Paste command will position a copy of the selected objects in the centre of the new layer; whilst the Paste in Place option keeps the relative position of the objects on the layer. Examples of both cases are shown in Figure 8.8. Once the objects are on the new layer, we can adjust the positions as required by selecting the objects and dragging them.

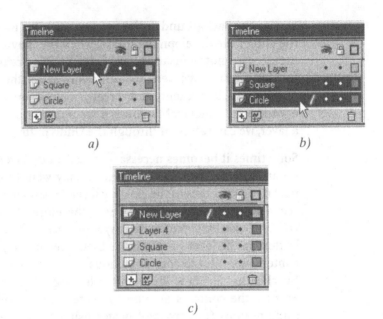

a)　　　　　　　　　　*b)*

c)

Figure 8.6 *Copying a block of layers: (a) creation of a new layer which represents the top layer for the pasted version, (b) selection of a block (Square and Circle) to be copied, and (c) effect of pasting the block, where the New Layer contains the contents of the Square layer and Layer 4 (which Flash automatically creates) contains the contents of the Circle layer.*

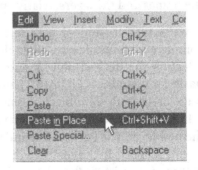

Figure 8.7 *Option of either copying through Paste or Paste in Place commands, found by choosing* Edit | Paste *or* Edit | Paste in Place, *respectively.*

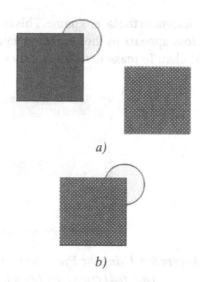

a)

b)

Figure 8.8 Illustration of the effect of copying an object from one layer to another (in this case the square) using: (a) the Paste command, and (b) the Paste in Place command.

Viewing layers

As our Flash movie develops, we will have created a number of layers to represent the scenes. Attempting to locate and edit the contents of individual layers can become rather cumbersome. The names of layers do help, but sometimes we would just want to see, for example, the objects belonging to a particular layer. There are four ways of highlighting the contents of a layer:

- hide the other layers (and therefore their respective contents),
- change contents to outlines,
- change the colour of outlines, or
- change the height of the layer in the layer interface and thus the Timeline.

We can hide a layer by using the Eye column on the layer interface. To hide a single layer, we simply click the Eye cell adjacent to the layer's name. This is shown in Figure 8.9. A red cross appears in the respective Eye cell to indicate that it is hidden. To make it visible, we click the Eye cell again.

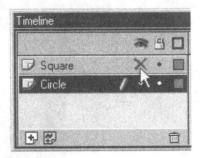

Figure 8.9 *Using the Eye column to hide and unhide a layer. The (red) cross signifies a layer that is hidden.*

We can use the eye icon (top of the Eye column) to hide all layers. Again, we can click to hide and click once more to unhide. This is demonstrated in Figure 8.10.

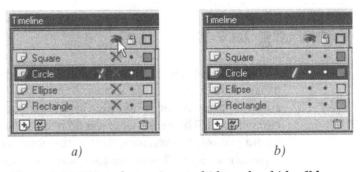

Figure 8.10 *Using the eye icon to hide and unhide all layers: (a) click once to hide, and (b) click again to unhide.*

To hide a block of layers, we select the Eye cells of the layers in question. As we drag through the Eye cells, they toggle from unhide to hide. The process is animated in Figure 8.11. We can return to the show (or unhide) state by dragging through the Eye cells of the desired layers. There is also a quicker way of hiding all other layers apart from the selected one. This way, we will only see the objects belonging to the selected layer. In this case, we use the combination of Alt and click to toggle between hide all except one and to show all. As Figure 8.12 shows, we employ this combination on the Eye cell of the desired layer.

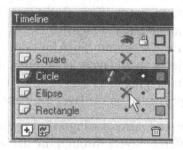

Figure 8.11 *By selecting Eye cells belonging to a block of layers, we can switch between hide and unhide modes for these.*

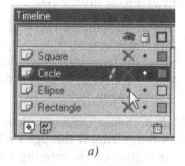

a)

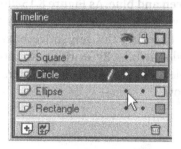

b)

Figure 8.12 *Using Alt and click combination allows one layer to be only visible: (a) hiding all layers except the one (Ellipse) selected, and (b) reverting to show all through using the same combination.*

At times, we may not want to hide a layer but simply have its contents appear in another form so that we can work with the intended layer and keep the others as a reference. Flash provides another column within the layer interface which converts the objects belonging to the selected layers to outline form. The Outline column and its effect are demonstrated in Figure 8.13. The way this operates is similar to the Eye column. So if, for example, we wanted to display all objects on all layers as outlines, we would click the Outline icon. Figure 8.14 shows how a layer in outline mode is represented on the layer interface.

We can also distinguish between outlines belonging to different layers through the use of colours. Outlines for one layer could be red, whilst for another layer blue, and for the third layer green. We set the colour of outlines for a layer via the Layer Properties dialogue box. This can be opened in any of the following three ways:

- double-click the icon on the left of the layer name, on the layer interface,
- select the layer and choose `Modify | Layer to`, or
- right-click the layer name and choose Properties from the context menu.

We then choose Outline Colour to specify a colour from either the palette, or through clicking the appropriate Color Picker button, or via entering a hexadecimal value for red, green and blue. As Figure 8.15 illustrates, we can also choose to view the respective layer in outline mode, or even hide it by checking the respective boxes in the Layer Properties dialogue box. By working in outline mode, we can edit the objects as before, the only difference being that fills will not show.

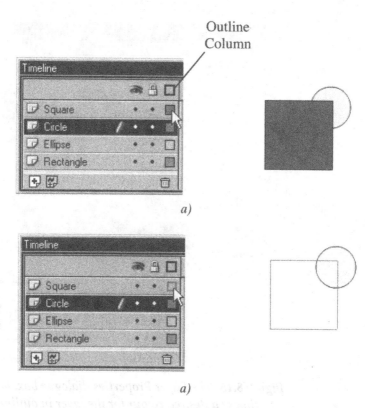

a)

a)

Figure 8.13 *Converting contents of objects to their outline form: (a) original (square) object, and (b) object in outline form.*

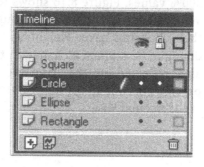

Figure 8.14 *Example of all layers in outline mode, where the icon under the Outline column has changed to show no fill (that is, outline only).*

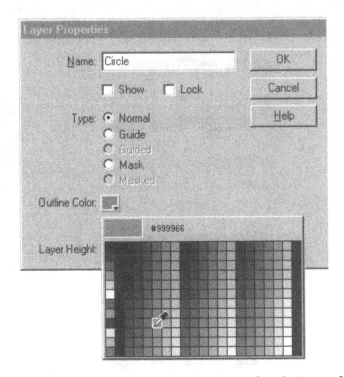

Figure 8.15 *The Layer Properties dialogue box, being used to choose a desired colour for the layer in outline mode.*

The fourth way of highlighting a layer is through changing its height. We have a choice of working with 100%, 200%, or 300% values. Figure 8.16 shows the corresponding result. We can specify the height through selecting a layer and then choosing Layer Height within the Layer Properties dialogue box. Since a change in the height of the layer is also reflected in the Timeline, it is a useful way of previewing contents of frames which may be difficult to see at the normal size.

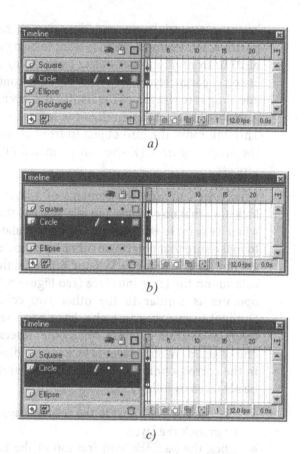

Figure 8.16 *Working with different heights for a selected layer: (a) 100%, (b) 200%, and (c) 300%.*

The layer interface displays all layers for a given scene. We can control the number of layers displayed by dragging the bar that separates the Timeline from the Stage. This is illustrated in Figure 8.17. As we can also see from this, a vertical scroll bar is attached to the Timeline if the number of layers exceeds the display window.

As mentioned earlier, layers are arranged in a stacking order. The order is based on the insertion of a new layer. That is, when a new layer is created, it is positioned above the current active layer. As the movie develops, however, we may wish to re-arrange the order. This is achieved through selecting a layer or several layers and dragging them to their new position. For example, we may want to bring an object (say, a bird) in front of another object (say, a tree). Assuming both are on separate layers, we select the layer containing the bird and drag it to the top of the list (in the layer interface) or at least to a higher position than the layer containing the tree. This will move the bird object in front of the tree object on the Stage. Figure 8.17 gives an animated illustration of the process.

Finally, we can view the contents of a layer but have them locked so that no changes can take place to them. This is ideal when we want to edit contents of a particular layer and want to make sure that objects on other layers are not accidentally altered. Layers can be locked and unlocked through the Lock column on the layer interface (see Figure 8.1). The way this operates is similar to the other two columns (Eye and Outline) in that we can lock a layer or all layers, a block of layers, a selection of layers, or all other layers apart from the one selected. When a layer is locked, a padlock icon appears in the corresponding Lock cell. Locking and unlocking can be achieved as follows:

- Use the Lock cell next to the selected layer's name to lock or unlock the layer,
- Click the padlock icon (on top of the Lock column) to lock or unlock all layers,
- Drag through the Lock column to lock a block of layers, or
- Alt and click the Lock cell of a desired layer to lock all other layers apart from this one.

Figure 8.18 gives an illustrative example of each of these cases. It should be noted that we could use a combination of Eye, Lock or Outline for selected layers, so that a layer could be in outline mode and also be locked at the same time. In addition, locking, outlining or hiding layers does not affect the final Flash movie. It will show the full contents, including fills.

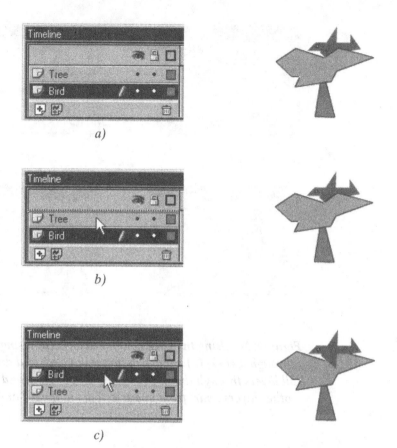

Figure 8.17 *Changing the order of layers and the effect on the Stage: (a) original, with the Bird behind the Tree, (b) moving the Bird layer to the top of the stacking order, and (c) the Bird layer on top of the stacking order: it now appears in front of the tree on the Stage.*

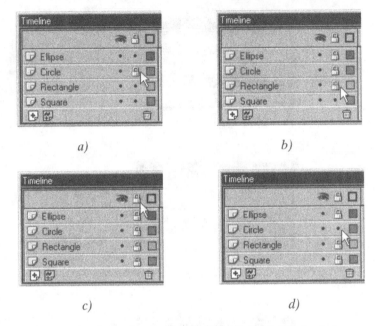

Figure 8.18 Using the Lock column to lock: (a) a single layer through a click, (b) a block of layers via click and drag, (c) all layers through the Lock column header icon, and (d) all other layers apart from one selected, via the Alt and click combination.

Types of layers

Flash works with five types of layers. These can be found in the Layer Properties dialogue box and an example of this is shown in Figure 8.19. As Figure 8.19 shows, the five types of layers are:

- Normal
- Guide
- Guided
- Mask
- Masked.

Typically, we are in Normal mode where the contents of the layer appear on the Stage. Then follows the Guide layer. This is where the layer in question acts as a style sheet or a template for other layers. In other words, this type is useful for establishing a desired layout for a scene. Other layers can use this to position the objects on the Stage. Multiple Guide layers can be used for a given scene or a Flash movie. The added benefit of using Guide layers is that they do not appear in the final, exported, movie.

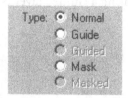

Figure 8.19 *Section of the Layer Properties dialogue box covering the five types of layers.*

Any layer can be changed to be a Guide layer. To make a layer a Guide layer (or to revert back to Normal type):

- Select the layer and right click for the context menu, and
- Then choose Guide.

A Guide layer is indicated on the layer interface by a new icon to the left of the layer's name. As Figure 8.20 shows, the icon for a Guide layer has two lines that are intersecting. We may want to rename the layer to reflect the type of guide, or turn on the Snap option (via View | Snap) to ensure objects follow the desired layout, or even use it as a means of viewing a movie without the layers that have changed to being guides.

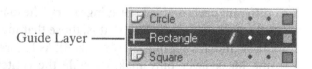

Figure 8.20 *An icon of two intersecting lines appears for a Guide layer, to the left of the layer's name on the layer interface.*

The third type of layers is listed as Guided and refers to layers which act as guides for motion and animation. Often called motion guide layers, they distinguish themselves from the Guide layers in that they are included in the exported Flash movie and are employed to provide a path for a ball bouncing, for example, across the Stage. So, their role is more dynamic than the Guide layer. Figure 8.21 shows that the icon highlighting a Guided layer is like an arch.

Guided Layer ———

Figure 8.21 *The icon of an arch shows a Guided layer, which is used to control the movement of objects (in this case, objects on the Car layer).*

A Guide layer can become a Guided (motion guide) layer if an existing Normal layer is dragged onto it. As more layers are created, this can happen unintentionally. To prevent this, we could re-arrange the ordering of the layers so that Guide layers are grouped and appear near the end of the stacking order. Further discussion on the Guided layer can be found in chapter 9, where we also look at creating motion in a scene.

We will look at the Mask and Masked types of layers together. A Mask layer has viewing holes through which we can see the contents of the underlying layer or layers. The latter are referred to as being Masked. In other words, the Mask layer acts as a viewing filter to the contents of layers behind it. What is more, is that the mask (that is, the viewing hole) can be dynamic so that it moves around the Stage to show different parts of the underlying layers. The mask works with all layers that are linked (that is, those that make use of this mask and are appropriately masked). As Figure 8.22 depicts, the Mask layer only makes visible the contents of linked (masked) layers that correlate with its viewing holes. Anything outside the viewing holes is filtered out.

We can generate a mask effect through the following steps:

- Select or create a Masked layer whose contents are to be made visible through the Mask layer.
- Create a new layer above the Masked layer, through using the Add Layer button. This will contain the viewing holes and generally is always above the Masked layer. Other layers can also be linked to this Mask layer.
- Next, draw the viewing holes on the Mask layer (that is, on the new layer that has been created in the previous step). These can be filled shapes, or an instance of a symbol, or some text. Filled areas act as transparent viewing windows, whilst unfilled sections of the Mask layer are opaque. Colours, line styles, transparency, gradients and bitmaps are ignored in a Mask layer.
- Convert the new layer containing the viewing holes to a Mask type. Here, we can either use the Layer Properties dialogue box or the contextual menu. Choosing the latter, we right-click on the layer's name and then select Mask from the context menu. Figure 8.23 provides an illustration of this.

As implied in the above steps, any layer immediately below the Mask layer is linked to it. On the layer interface, the Mask layer has a downward arrow as an icon, whilst the Masked layer has its name indented with a right-pointing arrow. Figure 8.24 gives an illustration of this.

Additional layers can be linked to the Mask layer by any of the three ways highlighted below:

- Drag an existing layer immediately below the Mask layer,
- Create a new layer anywhere below the mask layer, or
- Change the type of an existing layer to that of Masked.

To view the masking effect, we will need to lock the Mask layer and all linked layers. We can lock layers manually as described earlier or through using the context menu for the Mask or Masked layers. As Figure 8.25 demonstrates, the context menu has an option of Show Masking which, when selected, turns on the masking effect. We can also use Alt and click to toggle a layer between Masked and Normal modes. An animated example of the impact of masking on a scene is shown in Figure 8.26.

Masked layers can be unlinked from the mask by either changing their type from Masked to Normal (through Modify | Layer) or through dragging the Masked layers above the Mask layer. These layers can be hidden to assist the editing of objects or masks. In addition, we can have all linked layers revert to Normal if we delete the Mask layer.

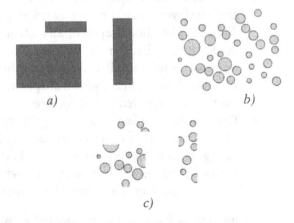

a)   *b)*

c)

Figure 8.22 *Shows the workings of a mask: (a) contents of the Mask layer, (b) contents of the Masked layer, and (c) the Mask layer makes visible only those parts of the Masked layer that correlate with its holes (contents).*

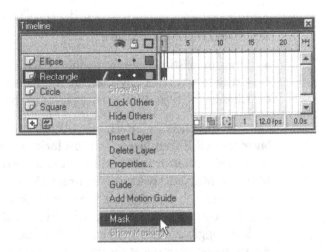

Figure 8.23 *Changing layer type to Mask through the context menu.*

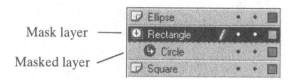

Figure 8.24 *Icons representing the mask and masked layers.*

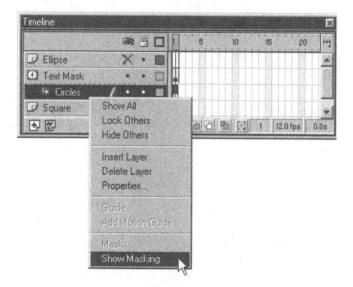

Figure 8.25 *Show Masking being used to activate the masking effect.*

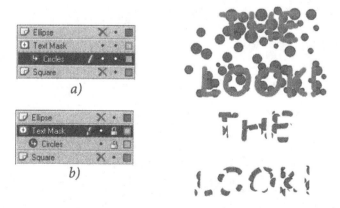

Figure 8.26 *Effect of locking and switching on the masking effect: (a) Mask and Masked layers before the masking has been activated, and (b) the scene after the masking has been activated. Note in the layer interface, both the Mask and Masked layers are locked to show the masking effect.*

Introduction

Chapter

9

Adding Animation

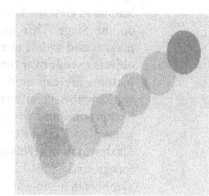

Introduction

We have seen in the previous chapter that objects on a Stage can be made multi-dimensional through the use of layers. Indeed, layers provide a flexible way of adding depth to a scene. When we work with different layers to form a scene, in fact, we are creating a single frame for our movie. This frame can, therefore, consist of a simple scene that involves an object or a few objects, or it can be more complex, which does not just have lots of objects, but also makes use of many types of objects that appear on several layers.

Working with a single frame, however, leaves one important aspect out and that is motion. This is where we use more than one frame to gain the illusion of movement. For example, if we had a filled circle on the first frame and we used an instance of the object on our second frame at a slightly adjusted position, then when we play the movie, we would see the filled circle moving. Using several frames in the same manner by adjusting the relative positions each time could lead us to view the filled circle as a ball being bounced about on the Stage. This has been a traditional ploy by movie makers and artists to create motion, where the attributes of objects change over time. In the case of the former, a series of pictures are captured to produce a video, whilst the artist works with several scenes using different layers to represent background and foreground objects to produce a cartoon animation. This latter approach correlates well with the way Flash works in terms of layers (which can be used to create foreground and background scenes), and instances of symbols that allow for characters to be re-usable so that their attributes can be adjusted as desired over several frames.

In this chapter, we look at the way Flash allows for the generation of animation through changing the content of successive frames. As an object moves across the Stage, it can change colour, shape, size, orientation, become more transparent or opaque, etc. We will look at the two approaches used to create animation: frame-by-frame and tweened. The former works by creating a scene for each frame, whilst the latter requires a start and an end frame and the in-between frames are generated automatically by Flash. We will begin by looking at the Timeline since this is pivotal to creating and editing animations.

Working with the Timeline

The Timeline is the lifeline for animation. This is where the dimension of time (and therefore motion) is inserted into a movie. We have already seen the value of layers to create a scene. For a given frame, we can use hundreds of layers to develop a complex scene. Moreover, we can split our animation or the number of different animations so that they occupy different layers. This way, we can edit and make adjustments without the complication of interference with other objects (since the latter can be locked and hidden). Figure 9.1 shows the Timeline with reference to it being used to create our animation.

As Figure 9.1 depicts, there are three primary sections to the Timeline. These are the layers, frames and the playhead. We have already looked at the layer interface and know that it resides to the left side of the Timeline. The corresponding frames for each layer appear to the right of the layer interface. The playhead indicates the position of the active frame (henceforth referred to as the current frame). The frame number is indicated within the header of the Timeline. The playhead scans across this header (in other words, the frames) to playback the contents of each frame for a given movie clip. We can view the contents of a frame by positioning the playhead on it and thus making it the current frame. Its contents then appear on the Stage. To go to a desired frame, say frame 10, we would use the Timeline header and click on 10. As Figure 9.2 demonstrates, this would take us to frame 10. We can also centre the playhead at the middle of a movie by choosing the button option shown in Figure 9.3. In addition, the playhead can be manually dragged to the right or left to respectively playback a movie's contents either in the forward or reverse direction.

At the bottom of the Timeline is the status line. This holds information about the current frame, the frame rate and the amount of time elapsed. The current frame is indicated by its frame number, which in turn shows the position of the playhead. The frame rate value shows the number of frames per second that have been set by using the Movie Properties dialogue box or, when in playback mode, the number of frames per second being played. The time elapsed gives a measure in seconds between the first frame and the current frame.

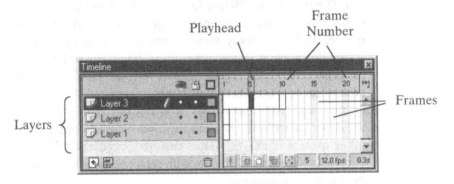

Figure 9.1 *The Timeline components which aid the development of animation.*

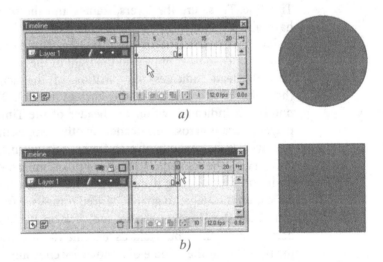

Figure 9.2 *Use of the playhead to view the contents of a desired frame: (a) frame 1, containing a circle, and (b) frame 10, containing a square.*

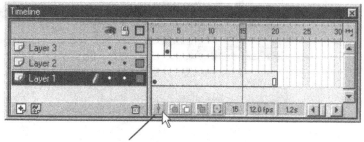

Centre Stage Frame

Figure 9.3 Using the Center Frame button to place the playhead at the middle of the movie.

The Timeline, in fact, is a separate window which can be docked so that it is seen to be attached to other parts of the Flash development environment. We can dock or move the Timeline by simply clicking and dragging it to the desired position (as outlined in chapter 1). We have already seen in the previous chapter that the number of layers (that is, the height of the Timeline) can be increased or decreased by dragging the bar separating the Timeline from the Stage. In addition, we can resize the Timeline, if it is not docked, by using any of the four corners. Figure 9.4 gives an illustration for using the bottom-right corner for this. Furthermore, we can shorten or lengthen the layer name fields (and thereby the number of frames that are visible) by dragging the bar separating the layer interface and the frames section of the Timeline. This is shown in Figure 9.5.

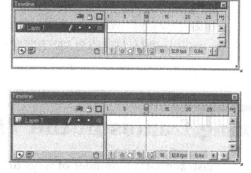

Figure 9.4 Use of the bottom-right corner to resize an undocked Timeline window.

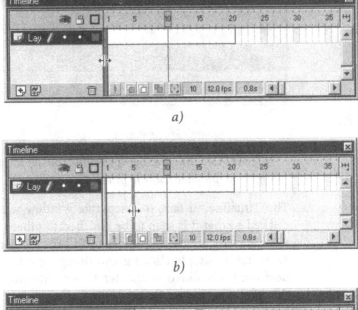

Figure 9.5 *Scaling the width of the two sections for the Timeline (layer interface and frames display) by dragging the bar separating both: (a) selection of separation bar, (b) move to increase layer width (and therefore decrease frame display width), and (c) result of movement of the separation bar.*

Viewing frames in the Timeline

Flash supports a number of ways to view the frames in the Timeline. Sequences of frames can be viewed with tinted cells or, better still, the frames can include thumbnail previews of the frame content. We can use these and other display options through using the Frame View button located on the top right corner of the Timeline. As Figure 9.6 shows, this opens a pop-up menu of viewing options. The way these work is listed below:

- Tiny, Small, Normal, Medium and Large refer to the width of the frame cells. The large size is useful for viewing sound waveforms.
- Short is used to reduce the (row) height of frame cells.
- Tinted Frames provides a way of differentiating between a series of frames through using different shades of colour.
- Preview and Preview in Context return thumbnails of the contents of each frame. Preview leaves the frame size unchanged, so that Flash scales the contents to fit the frame dimensions. Preview in Context is similar to the Preview option except that the contents of frames are relatively smaller. This is useful for seeing how the contents of a movie span across several frames.

Illustrated in Figure 9.7 are the affect of using Tiny, Small, Normal, Medium and Large sizes. Figure 9.8 shows the workings of the Short, Tinted Frames, Preview and Preview in Context options.

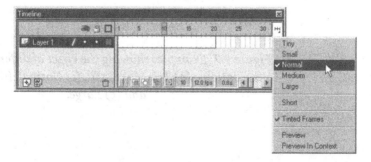

Figure 9.6 *Pop-up menu for viewing and resizing frames, activated by the Frame View button.*

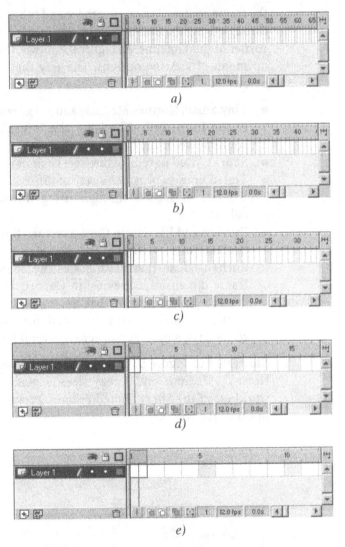

Figure 9.7 *Examples showing the effect of different Frame View options: (a) Tiny, (b) Small, (c) Normal, (d) Medium, and (e) Large.*

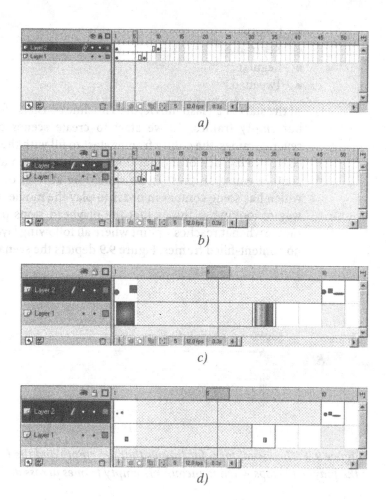

Figure 9.8 Illustrations showing changes in frame height, colour and thumbnail previews through the respective options on the Frame View menu: (a) Short, (b) Tinted Frames, (c) Preview, and (d) Preview in Context.

Frame types

There are effectively four types of frames that Flash works with. Their appearance on the Timeline is slightly different to distinguish them from each other. The four types are:

- Empty
- Keyframe
- Regular
- Tweened.

At the start of a Flash movie, the Timeline consists of nothing but empty frames. As we start to create scenes covering several frames, the empty frames start to fill with the desired content. Playback of movies does not occur when all layers contain empty frames. There should be at least one frame which has some content in order to play the movie. Another way of looking at this is that the playhead stops playing a movie when it reaches a point where all following layers have no content-filled frames. Figure 9.9 depicts the scenario.

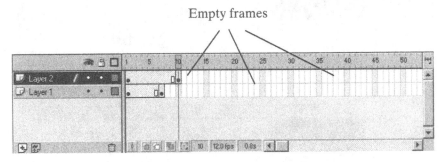

Figure 9.9 *The visual form for frames that are empty and the fact that the playhead stops when it encounters empty frames across all layers.*

Keyframes are the most important type when it comes to using them to develop an animation. The name suggests something special about them and, indeed, their usage is distinct. Keyframes are introduced in a movie when there is some change in the scene. Change could be in the form of object attributes such as colour or size, or editing an object's shape or its action. The number of keyframes employed in a movie will depend on the contents of the movie and the type of animation used. Tweened animation, for example, requires only two keyframes, one at the start and the other at the end. Flash can automatically work out the contents of the in-between frames.

There are three types of keyframes: blank, regular and one that has some action attached to it. The visual forms for these are shown in Figure 9.10. Whenever we start a new movie, a blank keyframe is automatically created in the first frame of layer 1.

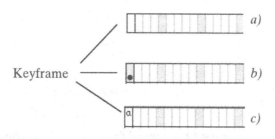

Figure 9.10 *Three types of keyframes: (a) blank, (b) regular, and (c) an attached action.*

In-between or regular frames are those frames that usually occur after a desired keyframe. The content of these is related to the keyframe and provides a useful way of adding a backdrop to a movie covering several frames (until the regular frames come across the next keyframe). Keyframes that have a content return regular frames which are slightly grey shaded, whilst blank keyframes yield white regular frames that follow them. Note that a hollow rectangle appears in the last frame of the span if there is no keyframe at the end. Figure 9.11 gives an example of these cases.

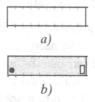

Figure 9.11 *Regular, in-between, frames are shown differently on the Timeline depending upon the type of keyframe preceding them: (a) blank keyframe, and (b) regular keyframe.*

Tweened frames come in two types: motion or shape. Both work with keyframes at both ends of an animation. As Figure 9.12 shows, the distinguishing visual feature on the Timeline is the different shading used for the in-between frames. In fact, shape-tweened uses light green, whilst motion-tweened has light blue. Tweened animation is looked at in greater detail in the latter half of this chapter.

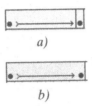

Figure 9.12 *Tweened frames: (a) shape (light green shaded), and (b) motion (light blue shaded).*

Working with frames

Flash provides a number of options when it comes to working with frames. These can be summarized as follows:

- Frames can be inserted, deleted, selected and dragged to a new location on the same layer or on a different layer.
- They can be copied and pasted as desired.
- Frame types can be converted, say, from regular frame to keyframe.
- An item can be added to the current keyframe by dragging its instance from the Library onto the Stage.

We can insert a new (in-between) frame by choosing Insert | Frame. This will insert a blank frame at the location of the current frame. We can also choose to insert keyframes. Flash offers two options for this: Insert | Keyframe and Insert | Blank Keyframe. The difference between the two is that the former option inserts a new keyframe whose contents are the same as the previous keyframe in the layer. This is useful if we intend to make minor adjustments to the contents. Inserting a blank keyframe, on the other hand, yields a keyframe which is empty. As Figure 9.13 depicts, these options can also be activated through using the context menu (through right-clicking at the location on the Timeline where a new keyframe is required). An illustrative example of each case is given in Figure 9.14.

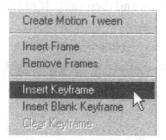

Figure 9.13 Context menu for frames, where options for creating keyframes are provided.

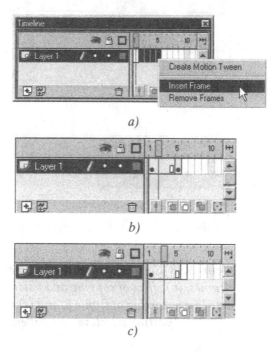

Figure 9.14 Examples of inserting frames: (a) four regular (in-between) frames, (b) an end keyframe, which will have a copy of the preceding keyframe, and (c) an end blank keyframe, which is empty.

By selecting a frame or a series of frames (including keyframes), we can choose to delete them from the Timeline through Insert | Remove Frame or via the context menu. Frames can also be copied and pasted on the same or a different layer. Figure 9.15 depicts both cases where we use Edit | Copy Frames and then Edit | Paste Frames to achieve this.

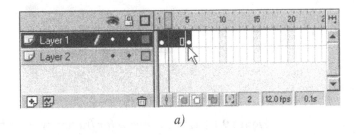

a)

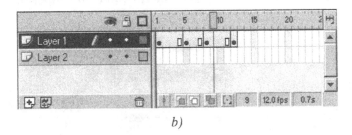

b)

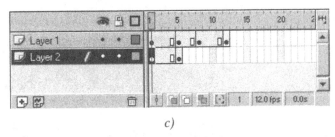

c)

Figure 9.15 *Copying and pasting frames: (a) selection of 5 frames, (b) effect of copying and pasting selection on the same layer, starting at frame 8, and (c) effect of copying and pasting selection on a different layer.*

Moving frames is similar to moving objects on the Stage since we select the desired number of frames and drag them to their new position. Figure 9.16 gives an illustration of this.

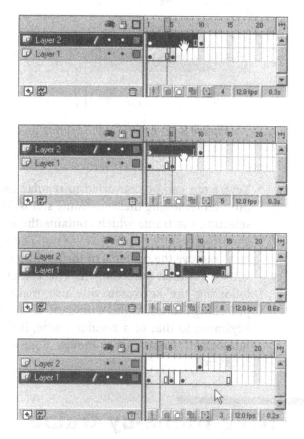

Figure 9.16 *Moving frames between layers (from Layer 2 to Layer 1).*

The duration of a keyframe can be extended through a new series of regular frames. For this, we would use Alt and click to drag the respective keyframe to attach to the regular frames. This is demonstrated in Figure 9.17.

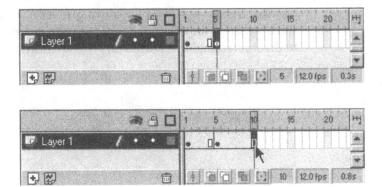

Figure 9.17 *Extending the duration of a keyframe by Alt-click and drag.*

Keyframes can be converted to regular, in-between, frames through removing their keyframe status. This is achieved by selecting the frame which contains the keyframe and then choosing Insert | Clear Keyframe. The effect of this would be to remove the contents of the keyframe and replace them with the frame preceding it. The contents of the frames following the keyframe will also make reference to the preceding frames. As this command changes the status of the keyframe to that of a regular frame, it does not affect the number of frames in a movie. Figure 9.18 depicts this scenario.

Creating frame-by-frame animation

As the name suggests, we work with a series of frames to generate this type of animation. In essence, a number of keyframes are used to capture the changing nature of the animation. We start by defining a keyframe within a layer and then its contents on the Stage. Having produced the contents for the first keyframe, we next add a new keyframe to the right (and on the same layer) of the first. Flash automatically copies the contents of the first keyframe to the second. We can

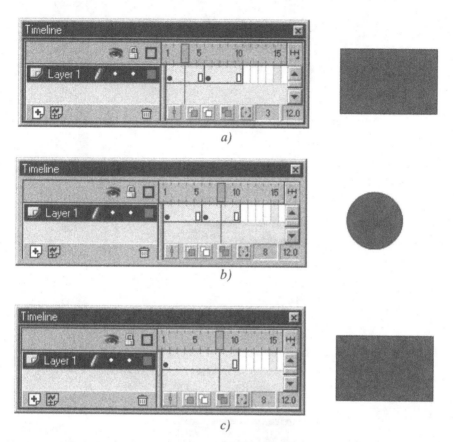

Figure 9.18 *Conversion of a keyframe to a regular frame: (a) frames 1 to 5 contain a rectangle, (b) frames 6 to 10 contain a circle, and (c) removal of the keyframe (frame 6) causes the first sequence to extend across frames 6 to 10.*

then make changes to the contents of the second keyframe to highlight the next phase in the animation. This process of keyframe insertion and editing of its contents continues until the full animation has been created. Figure 9.19 shows an example of a ball bouncing, created using three keyframes.

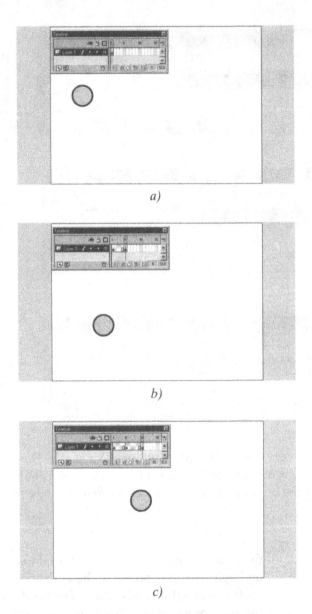

Figure 9.19 *Bouncing ball created using frame-by-frame animation: (a) creation of a ball object in the first keyframe, (b) shifting the object to a new position in the second keyframe, and (c) final position of the ball object in the third keyframe.*

We can play an animation through using either the Play button on the Controller window or Control | Play. This provides one way of testing an animation. As Figure 9.20 depicts, alternative ways include using Control | Step Forward or Control | Step Backward to look at the animation a frame at a time. The Control | Loop Playback provides a means of playing the finished animation repeatedly.

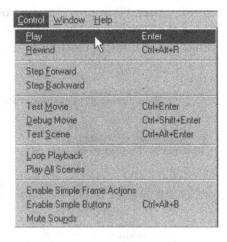

Figure 9.20 *The Control menu whose options can be used to test a movie.*

If we wanted to reverse the sequence of an animation, then this is also possible. We select the animation sequence from the Timeline and then choose Modify | Frames and then Reverse.

To smooth out the animation, we will need to use more keyframes so that the changes from frame to frame are relatively less. In the case of the example shown in Figure 9.19, we would insert more keyframes between frames 1 and 2, and then between 2 and 3. These would contain intermediate positions for the ball object, leaving the start and end positions the same. Overall, as we are using more frames, this increases the duration of the bouncing sequence and thus has the effect of smoothing out the animation.

Onion-skinning an animation

Creating an animation by using a series of frames works well, but for the case when editing of an object needs to be made with reference to the contents of other keyframes involved in the animation sequence. As it stands, we can use the Stage to view the contents of a single keyframe, but not the contents of several keyframes. To overcome this problem and to make editing easier, Flash provides a set of buttons on the status bar of the Timeline to onion-skin an animation. Figure 9.21 shows the position of these buttons on the Timeline.

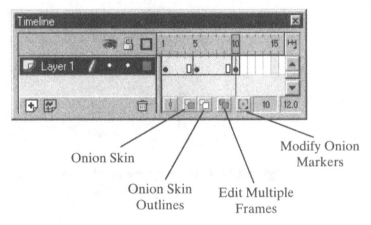

Figure 9.21 Onion-skinning buttons on the status bar of the Timeline.

The onion-skinning feature allows for the contents of a series of frames to be viewed on the Stage. The contents of the frame currently under the playhead are shown completely and can be edited. The contents of other frames in the animation are also shown but are dimmed. In analogy to onions, where the skin layers have different sizes and thickness, the amount of dimness varies from frame to frame, to show their relative positions to the keyframe under the playhead. The closer a keyframe is to the playhead, the darker the image. Figure 9.22 depicts the scenario.

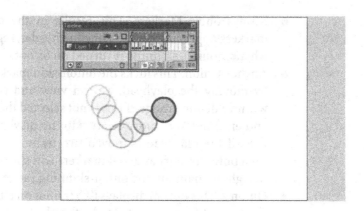

Figure 9.22 *Onion-skinning an animation, with varying levels of dimness in relation to the current frame.*

To turn on the onion-skinning effect, we use the Onion Skin button (see Figure 9.21). This then displays all frames which appear between the Start Onion Skin and End Onion Skin markers (which appear on the Timeline header). Figure 9.23 depicts an example.

Start Onion Skin   End Onion Skin

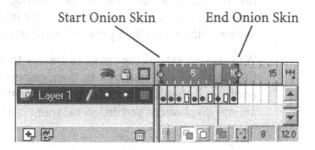

Figure 9.23 *Display markers used to specify the range for the onion-skinning.*

We can change the number of frames involved in the onion-skinning process through using the Modify Onion Markers button (see Figure 9.21). The button opens a pop-up menu which is shown in Figure 9.24. The list of options can be summarized as follows:

- Always Show Markers. This results in the onion-skin markers appearing on the Timeline header, regardless of whether onion-skinning is turned on or not.
- Anchor Onion. This locks the onion-skin markers so that by moving the playhead, we can view and edit frames within a defined range. If this is not selected the two (start and end) markers move relative to the playhead. In this case, if the playhead is moved two frames to the right, then both the start and end markers will shift two places to right to maintain the onion-skinning range.
- Onion 2. This option displays two frames on either side of the current frame, pointed to by the playhead.
- Onion 5. This allows for five frames to be displayed on either side of the current frame.
- Onion All. All frames on either side of the current frame are shown.

At times, it becomes necessary to edit a series of frames rather than a single frame in an animation. Flash provides the Edit Multiple Frames button (see Figure 9.21) which caters for this. The effect is to display the contents of all the frames that appear between the start and end markers. These can be edited as desired. To aid editing, the Onion Skin Outlines button can be used to show the outlines of objects, without fills. Figure 9.25 provides an illustrative example.

We can also extend the range of frames to edit by dragging the start and end markers to their respective positions. In addition, it should be noted that the contents of locked layers are not displayed when onion-skinning is activated.

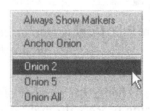

Figure 9.24 Menu associated with the Modify Onion Markers which is used to specify the range for onion-skinning.

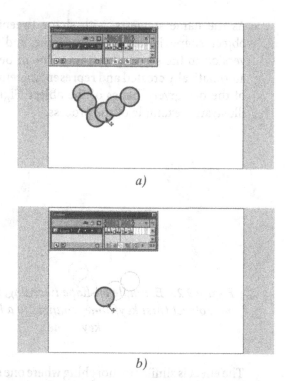

Figure 9.25 *Use of onion-skinning buttons: (a) Edit Multiple Frames, to modify a group of frames, and (b) Onion Skin Outlines, to remove fills of contents.*

Creating shape-tweened animation

We can work with frame-by-frame animation and create the desired effects. The manual nature of the approach, however, makes it difficult to represent complex animations. Having a lot of keyframes also leads to large file sizes. Flash provides an alternative approach for generating animations. This is referred to as tweening, where the start and end keyframes are defined and Flash automatically creates the in-between frames. There are two components to tweening: shape and motion. We will look at shape tweening in this section, whilst motion tweening is described in the next section.

As the name suggests, with shape tweening, we create an object shape in the first keyframe and then a modified version in the second keyframe. The in-between frames are automatically created and represent incremental interpolates of the two given shapes of the object. Figure 9.26 shows an illustrative example of the process.

Figure 9.26 Example of shape tweening, where the initial nail object (first keyframe) changes to a hook object (end keyframe).

The effect is similar to morphing where one shape changes into another. Although more than one object on a layer can be shape tweened (with unpredicatble results), bitmaps, text blocks, symbols and groups cannot be shape tweened. We can always use Modify | Break Apart on these objects and then apply shape tweening if required. Attribute changes of colour, size and location are permissible within this mode of animation.

The steps involved in creating a shape-tweened animation are as follows:

- Create an object within in your start keyframe.
- Decide upon the number of in-between frames required for the sequence and insert a new keyframe at the end of the sequence.
- Create a modified version of the object for the new, second, keyframe. Modification of shape, colour and position is allowed.
- Select the first keyframe and choose Window | Panels and then Frame. Click on the Tweening tab and choose Shape under Tweening. Figure 9.27 depicts the dialogue box.

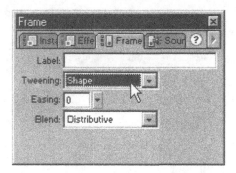

Figure 9.27 The Frame panel.

Figure 9.28 provides an illustrative example of shape-tweened animation. The first keyframe contains a circle and the last keyframe a square. The example makes use of 5 in-between frames. We can then choose the onion-skinning buttons to view the intermediate frames at the same time on the Stage. Here, we can use either the Onion Skin button (which will show any fills) or the Onion Skin Outlines button (which will only show objects as unfilled). In Figure 9.28, we show the effect of both cases.

We note from Figure 9.27 that we can specify the Blend Type and Easing for the shape-tweened animation. With Blend Type, we choose Angular if we wish to preserve sharp corners and straight lines when mixing objects belonging to the two keyframes takes place. Distributive, on the other hand, provides for a smoother transformation. The Easing option controls the speed of transformation. A zero value means that changes from one frame to the next will take place at the same rate. To begin the animation slowly and then to speed up, we either move the slider downwards or enter a value between -1 and -100 in the text box. If we wanted the opposite effect, then we would move the slider upwards or enter a positive value ranging from 1 to 100.

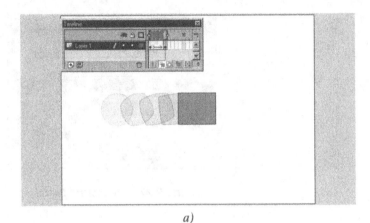

a)

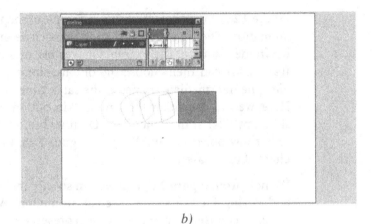

b)

Figure 9.28 *Shape-tweened animation, where the circle object changes into a square and occupies a new position on the Stage: (a) shown with Onion Skin button turned on, and (b) with Onion Skin Outlines button active.*

Sometimes it becomes necessary for the contents of the in-between frames to maintain certain characteristics of the objects appearing in the two keyframes defining the animation. Flash provides a way to assist the process of shape tweening so that a particular feature is maintained. Referred to as shape hints, there are 26 available for each tweened animation. Labels *a to z* are used for this purpose. It is good practice to use a convention for placing labels; for example, either clockwise or anti-clockwise. The ordering of placing labels in the first keyframe should match-up with the last keyframe.

We can use shape hints in the shape tweening animation through following the steps listed below:

- By selecting the first keyframe, choose Modify | Transform and then Add Shape Hints. A red circle with a letter *a* appears somewhere on the object. Drag and position the beginning shape hint (that is, the red circle with the letter *a*) to a desired edge or corner of the object.
- Select the last keyframe in the tweening sequence. A corresponding ending shape hint as a green circle with the letter *a* appears somewhere on the object. Move this to a place where it needs to match-up with the beginning shape hint (red circle with letter *a*).
- Test the animation to see the effect of introducing the shape hint and fine-tune positions to achieve the desired results.
- Introduce more shape hints by following the steps mentioned above.

Figure 9.29 shows the effect of introducing shape hints on a tweened animation. We can also view and hide shape hints. Through selecting a keyframe, we choose View | Show Shape Hints to display or to hide all shape hints associated with the keyframe. A shape hint can be removed by dragging it off the Stage. If we wanted to remove all the shape hints, then choosing Modify | Transform and then Remove All Hints can be used.

Creating motion-tweened animation

Motion-tweened animation works with instances, groups and text blocks. In this case, we can animate positions, sizes, and orientation (including skewing). Colour can also be

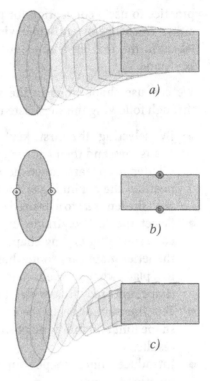

Figure 9.29 *Use of shape hints: (a) shape-tweened animation without shape hints, (b) introducing shape hints for the two objects in the first and last keyframes of the animation sequence, respectively, and (c) shape-tweened animation with shape hints.*

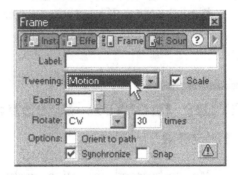

Figure 9.30 *Motion-tweening sub-options within the Frame panel.*

tweened, but groups of objects and text blocks will need to be converted into symbols first. Moreover we can create a path (straight or curved) for an object to follow.

Motion-tweened animation can be produced in two ways. The first is similar to the shape-tweening approach in that we create the start and end keyframes and then make use of the Frame panel. In this case, however, we choose Motion (instead of Shape) for the type of tweening required. The second way is to create the first keyframe and then choose Insert | Create Motion Tween. When the object, for example, is moved to a new location on the Stage, the end keyframe is automatically created by Flash. We look at both options below.

The following steps are used to create an animation using the Frame panel:

- Create a start keyframe containing an instance, group or text block on the Stage. Ensure that the object(s) in question has been converted to a symbol.
- Insert an end keyframe having a modified version of the contents for the start keyframe. The position of the end keyframe on the Timeline occurs after a desired number of in-between frames.
- Open the Frame panel (Window | Panels and then Frame) and click on the Tweening tab. Under the Tweening option, choose Motion. This results in the set of sub-options shown in Figure 9.30. The use of these depends on the nature of the animation and is discussed below.

The sub-options available within the Frame panel include Easing. This works the same way as for shape-tweened animation in that it offers the choice of accelerating or decelerating the start or end of an animation on playback. If the image in the second keyframe has been resized, then checking the Scale option will cater for this. Otherwise, constant size would be used throughout the animation. The Rotate option has a pop-up menu which allow for orientation as follows:

- None – no rotation
- Auto – allow rotation and work with direction that requires least motion
- Clockwise or CounterClockwise – rotate object in the direction chosen and as many times as indicated in the associated box. This would be in addition to any rotation that has been applied on the Stage to the modified version for the end keyframe. Figure 9.31 gives an illustrative example.

We can also create motion-tweened animation through using `Create Motion Tween` from the Insert menu. The steps for this are as follows:

- Draw an object or drag an instance from the Library on the Stage for the first keyframe.
- Next choose `Insert | Create Motion Tween`. This automatically converts any objects involved in the animation to symbols and assigns the names tween1, tween2, etc.
- Through selecting `Insert | Frame`, add an end frame for the animation at a desired location on the Timeline.
- Adjust position, size, orientation, etc., of the objects in the end frame to define the nature of the tween. Flash automatically adds a keyframe to the end of the animation sequence.
- The options on the Frame panel can then be used to fine-tune the tweening to meet a desired requirement.

Flash provides a novel way of defining motion paths for objects. Thus far, we have looked at moving objects effectively in a straight-line fashion. In the case of the

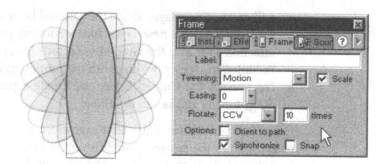

Figure 9.31 Rotating a motion-tweened object through using the Rotate option in the Frame panel in a counterclockwise direction.

bouncing ball scenario presented earlier, we moved the object from a stationary point so that it hit the 'ground' and then bounced off the ground to a new end position (see Figure 9.22). Both parts (before and after the contact with the ground) are defined using a straight-line path. This path, however, can be created so that objects travel in any desired manner within an animation. For this, we can use the pen, pencil, line, circle, brush or rectangle tools to generate a path.

The creation of what is referred to as the motion guide (that is, the path of travel) is done within an appropriately named layer: the Motion Guide Layer. A number of objects on different layers can be linked to a single motion guide layer. Alternatively, multiple motion layers can be used to support a number of normal layers. Layers linked to a motion guide layer are referred to as Guided Layers.

To apply a motion path to an animation, we first create a motion-tweened sequence using either of the two approaches outlined above. Having done this, we can follow the two steps listed below:

- By selecting the layer containing the animation choose either Insert | Motion Guide or Add Motion Guide from the context menu (gained by right-clicking), or click on the Add Motion Button located at the bottom right on the Layer interface (next to the Add Layer button). This will create a new layer above the selected layer. As Figure 9.32 depicts, the new layer has a motion guide icon attached to it and the Guided (selected) Layer becomes indented to signify the link with the motion guide layer.

- Next select the Guided Layer and create a path on the Stage for the animation to follow.

Figure 9.33 provides an illustrative example, where the (plane) object follows the created path. Within the Frame panel (see Figure 9.31), there are two options which come into play when working with motion paths. The effect of using the Orient to Path option can be seen by comparing Figure 9.33(c) (which does not orient to the path) with that of Figure 9.34 that forces the object to follow the curvature and slope of the defined path. From this, it can be seen that, for the example shown, Figure 9.33(c) provides for a more natural sequence. This, however, will depend on the contents and the type of animation effect being created, so in practice it is best to experiment.

Checking the Snap option on the Frame panel will ensure that the registration point of the tweened object follows the motion path. In addition, it will snap the respective objects (symbols and instances) on the two end keyframes to lie on the motion path.

There are four ways of linking normal layers (that is, converting layers into guide layers) to a motion guide layer:

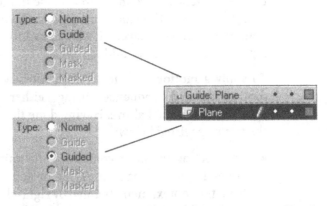

Figure 9.32 *A motion guide layer has a corresponding icon attached to it and any layers linked to it are shown indented.*

- Drag an existing layer below a motion guide layer
- Create a new layer below a motion guide layer
- Select a layer below a motion guide layer. Open the Layer Properties dialogue box (through Modify | Layer) and choose Guided under Type, or
- Alt and click the desired layer. This acts as a toggle to switch between normal and guided layer. So, clicking it again will reinstate the selected layer to a normal type.

Once a motion path has been created, it is best to lock the motion guide layer to prevent unintentional editing. Furthermore, we can use the Eye column (on the Layer interface) to hide the motion guide layer so that only the animation is visible when testing a sequence.

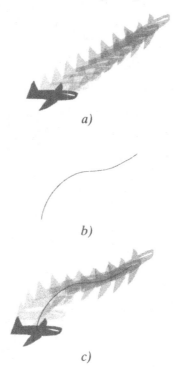

a)

b)

c)

Figure 9.33 Example of the use of a motion path to guide a plane object: (a) animation without a defined path – the straight line trajectory is based on the relative positional changes from the first keyframe to that of the end keyframe, (b) motion path, and (c) the effect of using the motion guide layer.

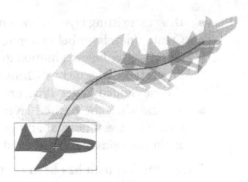

Figure 9.34 *Effect of choosing Orient to Path (from the Frame panel).*

Chapter
10

Interactivity
and Scripting

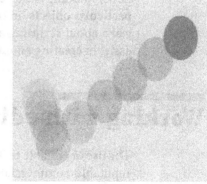

Introduction

Producing movies that grab the attention of an audience is not just an art, but a necessity in today's global market. Products sell when a client is attracted to them. Once fascinated, the client often wants to find out more about the product. For this to occur, dialogue needs to take place between the movie (that is, the product) and the user (that is, the client). Flash provides for this so that, instead of playing frames and scenes sequentially, it allows for users to interact with a movie. The mode of interaction can take several forms in terms of buttons placed within a scene to select from a list and hence the movement to a particular frame, or through assigning actions to frames. The latter, as we will see in this chapter, is achieved through a scripting language that Macromedia refers to as ActionScript. The desired action takes place when a particular event is activated.

This chapter starts with introducing editable text boxes which allow for dynamically updating text. We next look at understanding and employing actions in a movie; in particular objects on the Stage and frames. Through this we learn about scripting and how ActionScripts can be used to assist in creating an interactive movie.

Working with editable text boxes

The use of editable text boxes is not new. Browse through any reputable commercial web-site and you will come across either a form to complete or an area which is dynamically changing with information. Flash caters for both cases through the use of editable text boxes, available via the Text Options panel. This is activated by means of Window | Panels and then Text Options. As Figure 10.1 shows, this panel provides a number of options, including the type of text required. Dynamic Text provides for a text box whose information will automatically be updated, whilst Input Text refers to the user entering a value into the text box. Static text is the default and is used for creating a text block.

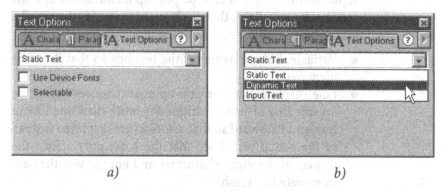

Figure 10.1 *Text Options panel: (a) full panel, and (b) showing the three types of text: Static, Dynamic and Input.*

If we choose Dynamic or Input Text, the Text Options panel shows the associated options for setting the appearance and controlling the text. Figure 10.2 shows the additional options for both cases. One of these is assigning a variable name. The variable name refers to the text field and provides a way of identifying it. This is a powerful feature which allows Flash to reference it so as to move it to another part of a movie or to another application. Moreover, the variable (that is, the text) can be updated dynamically. Here, for instance, if the Flash movie has been loaded in the browser then the editable boxes can be used to reflect the contents of a database. Changes in the database will be shown in the respective text box.

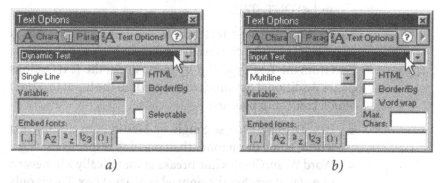

Figure 10.2 *Text Options panel for: (a) Dynamic Text and (b) Input Text.*

To create a text box to accept input from users (as in the case of forms), we open up the Text Options panel and choose Input Text from the Text Type pop-up menu. Seven options then become available that can be used to specify the way the text appears within a movie. The options are:

- Variable. Enter a name for the text box so that it can be identified
- Line Display. From the pop-up menu choose Single Line for one line of text, Multiline for more than one line of text, and Password so that asterisks are displayed instead of the actual text. Note that the latter only affects the display of the input characters and not the way they are interpreted by Flash.
- Draw Border and Background. Useful for specifying an outline and a background to the text box. This will make it stand out from other aspects of a web-page.
- Maximum Characters. Sets a limit to the number of characters that the user can enter in the text box.
- Embed Fonts. Allows for embedded characters and numbers to be used. Choose one or more, or all buttons to specify the characters to be embedded. The five buttons start from the bottom left (see Figure 10.2).
- HTML. When selected, this preserves the basic text formatting associated with HTML. Font name, style, colour and size, for example, are catered for by automatically applying the respective HTML tags to the text box. The HTML tags which are supported are: <A>, <B>, <I>, <P>, <U>, <FONT COLOR>, <FONT FACE> and <FONT SIZE>.

To create a dynamic text box where information such as share prices can be constantly updated, we choose Dynamic Text from the Text Type pop-up menu under the Text Options panel. Additional options (with regards to the input text box) which come into play are:

- Line Display. Choose Single or Multiline to display text within a line or on more than one line respectively.
- Word Wrap. Creates line breaks automatically whenever a line of text reaches the right edge of a text box. This is only valid if the Multiline option is active.

- Selectable. Allows for the text to be selected by users (as the default) or not to be selected.

We use `Control | Test Movie` to test the workings of both types. Both input and dynamic text boxes can have a variety of actions associated with them. We look at adding action to our movie in the following sections.

Introducing buttons

Actions can take various forms, though the underlying aspect is to allow the user some control over the movie that is being played and therefore to add interactivity. Interactivity itself is realized through events. Some action needs to take place to activate a change of some kind within a movie. This may be simply moving to a completely new scene. The event that initiates this could be user driven (that is, a mouse click or key press, or even a button within a menu). In other words, the user decides when and which scene to view. Alternatively, a new scene could be triggered by the passage of time. After a certain interval, a new scene appears. We refer to these as frame events, whilst user initiated actions are referred to as mouse/keyboard events.

The most popular form of interaction on web-sites is linked with having a menu with a set of options. By using a mouse click, a particular web-page or topic within a page is selected. In this case, a mouse event is interacting with a set of buttons (which are the menu options) to facilitate a dialogue. The buttons themselves are instances of symbols. Therefore, they can take any desired shape or form.

We create a button by using a symbol (or through creating a new image and converting it to a symbol) and assigning it the button behaviour within the Symbol Properties dialogue box. The effect of this is that on the Timeline, Flash creates four frames. This means that the button, in fact, is a four-frame interactive movie clip. The four frames in turn refer to Up, Over, Down and Hit states and are outlined below:

- First frame. Up state represents the button when the mouse cursor is not over the button.
- Second frame. Over state represents the button when the mouse cursor is over the button.
- Third frame. Down state represents the button when it is clicked.
- Fourth frame. Hit state represents the active boundary area for the button. This defines the region within which the mouse click will be recognized. It is invisible in the final movie.

To create a button, we will need to define contents for each of the four keyframes. The steps involved are as follows:

- We start with adding a symbol to the scene. Choose Insert | New Symbol. This opens the Symbol Properties dialogue box. Select Button as the Behavior and give the button a name. An example is shown in Figure 10.3.
- As Figure 10.4 depicts, four frames appear on the Timeline with headers of Up, Over, Down, and Hit respectively. Flash also switches to symbol-editing mode and points to the first frame (a blank keyframe). Create or import an appropriate button image for the Up state. A movie clip symbol can also be used.
- Select the second frame (headed Over) and convert it to a keyframe (right click and choose Insert Keyframe from the context menu). Flash automatically copies the contents of the Up state keyframe. Edit the button image for the Over state as desired.
- Repeat the above step for the Down and Hit frames.
- Place an instance of the button symbol from the Library onto the Stage.

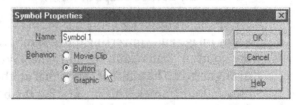

Figure 10.3 Symbol Properties dialogue box being used to create a button.

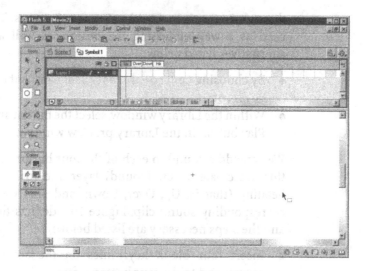

Figure 10.4 This shows the effect of choosing the button behaviour on the Timeline. It inserts four frames (Up, Over, Down, and Hit) and switches to symbol-editing mode.

As mentioned earlier, the Hit keyframe identifies an active area for the button. In other words, any mouse movements over this area will be interpreted as referring to the button. The area needs to be solid and also requires to cover all the three (Up, Over and Down) button images. We can use onion-skinning to view the contents of these frames so as to assist in ensuring the Hit keyframe covers all three states. The contents of the Hit keyframe are not visible on playback. If a Hit frame is not specified then the button image for the Up state is used to define the boundary. Figure 10.5 shows an illustrative example of creating a button; whilst Figure 10.6 shows its workings.

When creating and editing buttons, Flash, by default, disables them so that it is easier to work with them. This way, selecting a button will simply select the image associated with the button. When enabled, however, the button responds to the corresponding mouse event associated with it. In other words, the Over and Down states become visible if the mouse is respectively positioned and clicked. Buttons are enabled through `Control | Enable Simple Buttons`. This can be used as a way of testing the button, as well as the two alternatives listed below:

- By choosing `Control | Test Scene` or `Control | Test Movie`, or
- Within the Library window, select the button and click the Play button in the Library preview window.

We can add a sound to each of the four button states. To do this, we create a new (sound) layer and for each column heading (that is, Up, Over, Down, and Hit) we insert the corresponding sound clip. Figure 10.7 depicts the scenario and the steps necessary are listed below:

- Insert four blank keyframes on the sound layer to correspond to the four button states.
- Select the first keyframe (under Up state) and choose `Window | Panels` and then `Sound`. This will open up the Sound panel, an illustration of which is given in Figure 10.8. If no sound files are present then choose `Window | Common Libraries` and then `Sounds`. Select the desired sound clip from the Library (Sounds).
- Choose a sound file from the Sound pop-up menu.
- From the Synchronization pop-up menu, choose Event.
- Repeat the above steps for Over, Down, and Hit keyframes.

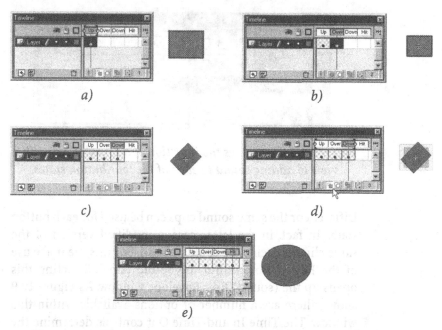

a)   b)

c)   d)

e)

Figure 10.5 *Example of creating a button: (a) contents of Up state, (b) contents of Over state, (c) contents of Down state, (d) use of onion-skinning to view frame contents to assist in generating the Hit frame, and (e) contents of the Hit state.*

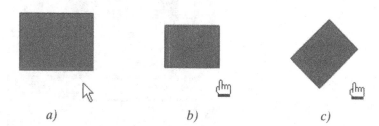

a)   b)   c)

Figure 10.6 *This shows the working of the button created in Figure 10.5. (a) Mouse cursor close to the button, but not within the Hit region. (b) Mouse cursor over the Hit region (rollover effect). (c) Mouse pressed.*

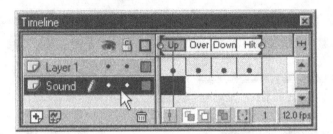

Figure 10.7 *This shows the insertion of a sound layer, with a view to adding sound to each of the four button states.*

Different or the same sound clips can be used for each button state. In fact, in the latter case, a modified version of the same clip for each state could be used. For this, we make use of the Edit option within the Sound panel. Selecting this opens up the (sound) Edit Envelope window. As Figure 10.9 shows, there are a number of options available within this window. The Time In and Time Out controls determine the start and end points for the sound clip. These are adjustable so that the four button states could be using the same sound clip, but different parts of it. Likewise, the envelope (which determines the volume) can be varied for each button state. Flash permits up to eight envelope handles. Figure 10.10 shows the insertion of sound clips for the button states, where a modified version of the same sound clip is used in each case.

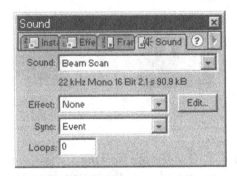

Figure 10.8 *The Sound panel.*

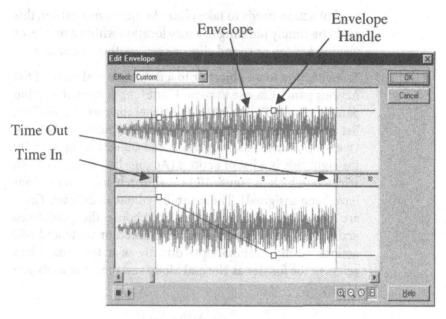

Figure 10.9 *Sound editing window which allows the start and end points,
as well as the envelope heights, to be adjusted.*

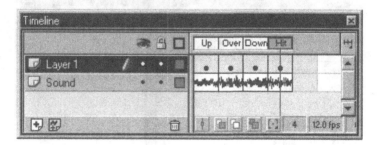

Figure 10.10 *The four button states are making use of the
same sound clip, but each having different starting points.*

Adding action to buttons

Having created the four states for the button, the next task is
to attach some action to them. For example, when the mouse
cursor is over the button, or when the button is pressed, some

kind of action needs to take place. As mentioned earlier, this could be simply jumping to a new location within a movie, or playing a video or sound clip, or even another animation.

To add action to an object or to a frame, we make use of the Actions panel. Choose Window | Actions to open the action panel shown in Figure 10.11. The panel consists of a Toolbox list on the left side that contains Basic Actions, Actions, Operators, Functions, Properties, and Objects categories. On the right side is a list of actions (Actions list) that have been selected (which in Figure 10.11 is shown blank as no actions have been assigned). These can be edited as desired. There are two ways of inserting action: choose the predefined actions and enter parameters as required or write and edit actions (using ActionScript) directly in a text box. Flash refers to the former as Normal Mode and the latter as Expert Mode.

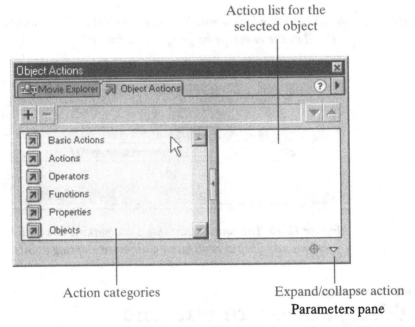

Action list for the
selected object

Action categories

Expand/collapse action
Parameters pane

Figure 10.11 *The Action panel for assigning actions to objects (as for buttons).*

Typically, we will be working in the Normal Mode to set actions for the buttons. Make sure this is set by viewing the pop-up menu associated with the Actions panel. The menu can be opened through clicking the arrow on the top right corner of the panel. To assign an action to the button, follow the steps listed below:

- Select an instance of the button, either from the Timeline or from the Stage. Ensure that you are in normal-editing and not in symbol-editing mode.
- Open Actions panel (by choosing `Window | Actions`).
- Click the Basic Actions category from the Toolbox list.
- Add an action through any of the following:
  - Double-click on the desired action (such as Go To)
  - Drag the desired action to the right side and placed it in the Actions list, or
  - Use the Add (+) button and select the action from the pop-up menu.
- If there are any parameters associated with the chosen action, then click on the triangle at the bottom right corner of the Actions panel to open the Parameters pane.
- Additional actions can be assigned by repeating the above steps.

When an action is assigned to a button, Flash automatically attaches a corresponding On Mouse Event handler. A handler contains groups of ActionScript statements which are executed when a desired event occurs. A handler for a mouse or keyboard begins with the word On, followed by the event which triggers the handler. The statement takes the form:

```
On (event)
  {(action)};
End On
```

The event in the case of a button, for example, can be the positioning of the mouse cursor over the button, or the button being pressed, or when it is released. The complete list is shown in Figure 10.12, where the parameters have the following meaning:

- Press. Initiates action when button is pressed.
- Release. Initiates action when button is pressed and then released. Flash uses this as the default setting.
- Release Outside. Initiates action when button is pressed, but released when cursor is not over the button.
- Key Press. Initiates action when the desired key is pressed. The desired key will need to be entered in the associated text box.
- Roll Over. Initiates action when mouse cursor appears across the Hit region.
- Roll Out. Initiates action when mouse cursor moves away from the Hit region.
- Drag Over. Initiates action when the button is pressed, the mouse cursor is then dragged off the Hit region (button) and then dragged back onto the button again.
- Drag Out. Initiates action when the button is pressed, and then the mouse cursor is dragged off the Hit region (button).

Figure 10.12 List of arguments available for On Mouse Event. With the Parameters pane active, double click on the line containing the event in the Actions list.

As a basic example, we can see that the following script will be executed whenever the respective button is pressed:

```
On (Press)
  { Play()};
End On
```

The action in this case is to Play(). This will start to playback a sequence so that the playhead moves forward in the Timeline. Other available actions include:

- GotoandPlay (scene, frame). Jumps to a frame within a scene or to a frame within another scene, and starts to play from the indicated frame.
- GotoandStop (scene, frame). Jumps to a frame within a scene or to a frame within another scene, and positions the playhead at the indicated frame.
- ToggleHighQuality. Switches between anti-aliasing on and off modes.
- StopAllSounds. Removes sound from a movie, without stopping the playhead.
- GetURL. Loads URL contents into a specified window. Can also be used to pass variables to the specified URL.
- LoadMovie. Loads additional Flash movies at a specified URL. Useful for displaying several movies at the same time, without opening another HTML document.

In addition, ActionScript allows for programming statements such as if and else, as well as a number of other well-known operators and statements like for loops to customize a movie. Choose Help | ActionScript Dictionary to view a full list of available commands and Help | ActionScript Reference to learn how to work with them.

Adding action to frames

Button actions require the user to trigger an event (mouse or key press) in order to generate an action. However, there may be instances where we may want some action to happen when the playhead reaches a particular frame within a sequence. For example, we have a scene which includes an animation that needs to make repeated appearances. In this case, we would want to play the animation, and when it reaches the end frame we would want it to start at the beginning again. To do this, we will need to insert an action in the end frame to tell it to loop back to the beginning. Let us see how we can do this.

We start by adding a new layer in the movie. This, as Figure 10.13 implies, will hold the actions for the frames and will assist in identifying the actions. The basic steps for assigning action to frames are the same as for buttons. So, we make use of the Actions panel (Window | Actions) and use the Toolbox list to add to the Actions list. Figure 10.13 depicts the scenario. It should be noted, however, that actions are assigned to keyframes and not to regular frames. Before commencing, therefore, ensure that the frame in question is a keyframe. If it is not, then Flash will automatically assign the action to the previous keyframe.

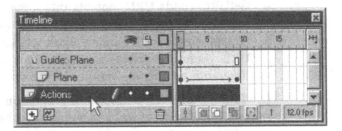

Figure 10.13 Addition of a new layer to hold frame actions.

Coming back to our example of wanting to loop back to the start of a sequence, we need to insert the action Go To at the end frame. This way, the playhead will be directed to the start frame and will begin playing, which is the default for this command. To aid clarity, we will insert a couple of labels for the start and end frames of the sequence. Frame labels are inserted using the Frame panel. Choose Window | Panels and then Frame to open up the panel. We next select the start and end frames and enter a label for each. Figure 10.14 shows the Frame panel with an entry for the label. The use of Frame labels is encouraged, as it not only aids clarity, but also assists in the editing of animation clips. If we decide to move the movie clip, for example, the labels stay with it. If, however, frame numbers were being used in the arguments for the actions, they will need to be adjusted. This can become tedious as more and more of a movie is created. Since labels are also exported with the movie, it is best to use labels with as few characters as possible to keep the filesize to a minimum. Figure 10.15 shows the effect of introducing the labels. Note that a new layer has been created to store the labels.

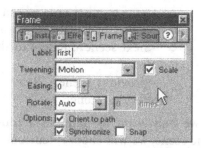

Figure 10.14 *The Frame panel being used to label a selected frame.*

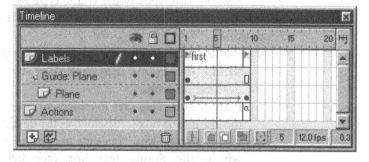

Figure 10.15 *Use of frame labels to identify frames within a movie. The labels are added within a new layer and their positions are indicated by a flag attachment in each case.*

To assign the action to the end keyframe, we do the following:

- Select the end keyframe, labelled 'last'.
- Open the Actions panel (choose `Window | Actions`). Double-click GotoAndPlay action under the Basic Actions category. This will add the action to the Action list and will play the sequence once it moves to the new destination (the 'first' frame).
- To specify the destination scene, we will need to open the Parameters pane within the Action panel. Having done this, we then click on the Scene option. Figure 10.16 depicts the scenario, where the following options for the scene are available:
  - o `<current scene>`. Refers to current scene where the frame number or label can be specified.
  - o Named_Scene. Refers to an alternative scene.
  - o `<next scene>`. Refers to the first frame of the next scene.
  - o `<previous scene>`. Refers to the first frame of the previous scene.

As we only want to jump to a frame which belongs to the same scene, we will choose `<current scene>`. Note also that the `<next scene>` and `<previous scene>` moves the playhead to the first frame in each case. If we wanted to move to different frame within another scene instead, we will use the Named_Scene option.

- Next, we need to specify the frame type within the Type text box. As Figure 10.17 depicts, this has the following options:
  - o Frame Number. This says to expect a frame number within the Frame text box (see below) as the destination point.
  - o Frame Label. This says to expect a frame label within the Frame text box (see below) as the destination point.
  - o Frame Expression. This says to expect an expression within the Frame text box (see below), whose evaluation will return a destination point.
  - o Next Frame. This has an effect of moving the playhead to the next frame within the same scene.

o   Previous Frame. This has an effect of moving the playhead to the previous frame within the same scene.

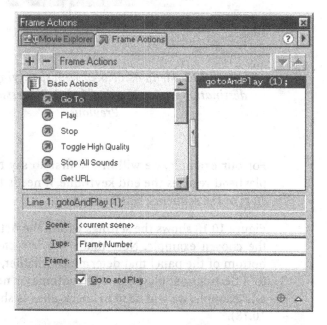

Figure 10.16 *Action panel for the last frame, with the gotoAndPlay command added to the Action list.*

We are using labels, so we will choose Frame Label here, though clearly we could have chosen Frame Number or Frame Expression to gain the same effect.

●   Finally, we will need to identify the frame destination in the Frame text box. What we enter here depends on the type of frame we have specified in the step above. This works for Frame Number, Frame Label or Expression. Examples of each are given below:

(Frame) Type text box	(Example entry for) Frame text box
Frame Number	4, 6, 27, 44, 82, etc
Frame Label	first, last, etc
Expression	_currentframe + 34, _currentframe - 15, etc

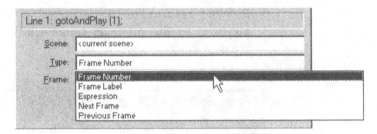

Figure 10.17 Menu associated with specifying the type of destination frame: Number, Label, Expression, Next or Previous.

For our example, we will insert 'first' to say that, when the playhead reaches the end keyframe, it needs to jump to the start of the sequence labelled as 'first'.

Figure 10.18 shows the settings within the Actions panel for the chosen example. Note that there is a checkbox at the bottom of the panel that determines whether, after jumping to a destination, playback will continue or not. Clearly, for our example, we will need to check this (as shown in Figure 10.18).

When working with a multi-layered frame, care must be taken to ensure that actions are allowed to be executed. This is because Flash uses a stacking order to determine which actions are executed first, for a given current frame. It always activates actions in the highest layer. If there are no actions associated with the top layer, it then moves down to the next layer. If there is an action associated with this layer, it is executed and the playhead moves on in the Timeline. In other words, if there were more than two layers then, in this case, actions assigned to layers below the second one will not be executed. So, the ordering of layers will have an impact on the way the movie plays.

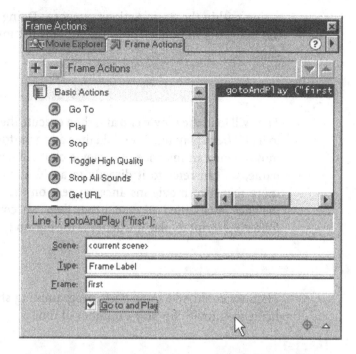

Figure 10.18 *Action panel settings for the end keyframe (labelled 'last' in Figure 10.15) so that the playhead jumps to the 'start' frame and continues to play.*

Working with movies

We assign actions to movie clips using the On Clip Event action. It works in a similar way to the On Mouse Event as discussed earlier, in that groups of ActionScript statements are executed when a specific event is triggered. In this case, the word onClipEvent is used instead of on to signify that we are dealing with a movie clip rather than a button.

Actions can be assigned to a movie clip using the same steps as for those outlined for buttons. We select an instance of the movie clip and then choose Window | Actions to display the Actions panel. If, for example, we wanted to load a movie and have it wait before playing then we would select the Stop action within the Basic Actions category. Doing so will add the following ActionScript in the Actions list for the movie clip:

```
onClipEvent (load)
{ stop (); }
```

This will load the movie clip and then execute the stop script to halt it from playing. We could then add a button to play the movie. Since an instance of a movie clip will have a unique name, we can refer to it directly to avoid any ambiguity if more than two movie instances appear on the Stage. If the instance was called flying_bird, then we could use the following script to play it whenever the button is pressed:

```
on (press)
{ flying_bird.play (); }
```

Then we could add some basic programming statements to make the movie clip play a number of times:

```
on (press)
{ count = 0;
  do
  { flying_bird.play ();
   count = count + 1;
  }
  while (count<3);
}
```

In this example, the movie clip will play for three times before the while condition is met.

We can also adjust the quality of a movie playback. Here, we allow the viewer to decide whether they want to view the movie using anti-aliasing or not. It is a question not just about the quality, but also the speed at which playback will occur. The process of anti-aliasing attempts to smooth out the edges of outlines by using a number of intermediate shades of colour (or levels of greys in the case of a black edge on a white background) that mirror the change in colour of the edge with the background. Calculating intermediate values takes a lot of processing time and thus has a deleterious effect on the playback speed. Through using the Toggle High Quality action, we can offer an option for the viewer to either switch the anti-aliasing on for high quality display or to turn it off for faster playback. To incorporate this option, we use the Action panel to insert the following ActionScripts:

```
on (release)
{  toggleHighQuality (); }
```

As we can see, the action is assigned to a button for a given movie clip and its effect takes place whenever the mouse button is pressed and then released. In other words, if the mouse button is pressed and then released, it will switch on anti-aliasing. Clicking the mouse button again will toggle the anti-aliasing option off.

Another useful action is Load Movie. This allows for several movies to be played at the same time, or for movies to be exchanged without closing the Flash Player, or having to load another HTML document. This may be useful, for example, if we want to play a sequence of banners in a specified region on the Stage (that is, web-page). In this case, we will want to load in a new movie clip at the end of the first clip and at the same position on the web-page. Alternatively, we may want to view more than one movie clip on a web-page. Load Movie caters for both cases. The steps involved are as follows:

- By selecting an instance (of a button, frame or movie clip) to which the Load Movie action will be assigned, choose Window | Actions to open the Actions panel.
- Select Load Movie action from the Basic Actions category within the Toolbox list. Figure 10.19 shows the scenario where the arguments for the Load Movie action can be seen having activated the Parameters pane.
- Options available in the Parameters pane include the following:
  - URL. Location of (swf, flash movie) file to be loaded. Can use relative or absolute address to specify location of file.
  - Location. Choose either Level or Target from the pop-up menu. Normally, a new movie is placed on a level and assigned a level number which identifies its

position. Movie clips, therefore, can occupy different levels (similar to objects placed on different layers). Level 0 represents the first movie clip and subsequent movie clips are placed on level 1, 2, 3, and so on. The first movie clip (at level 0) sets the frame rate, background colour and frame size for all movies loaded at other levels.

To replace an existing movie clip, we simply use the same level number that is currently occupied by another movie. Consequently, choosing a new level number (one that is not being used by any other loaded movie clip) will add the new movie to a new level. Figure 10.20 shows the case for loading a Flash movie (`ball.swf`) at level 2. Loading a movie clip at level 0 has the effect of replacing the first movie clip and unloading all others occupying other layers. Every movie clip that is loaded into a level has a corresponding Timeline.

Choosing Target allows for replacing an existing movie clip. This option will ensure that the loaded movie inherits all of the attributes belonging to the current movie. This includes name, position, rotation and scaling.

o Variable. Here, we have three options for sending variables belonging to the loaded movie to a server: Send Using Get, Send Using Post, or Don't Send. The former allows for small number of variables and appends these to the end of the URL, whilst Post sends variables separately from the URL and therefore is able to cater for a greater volume. Don't Send clearly prevents any variables from being passed.

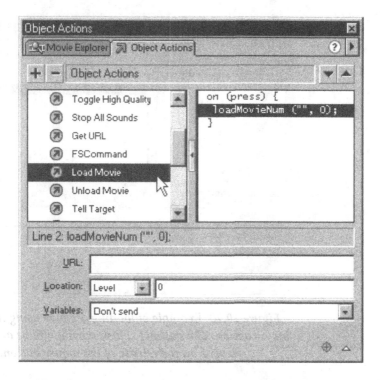

Figure 10.19 *This shows the Action panel for the Load Movie action.*

The process of unloading is similar to loading in that we choose the unLoadMovie action from the Toobox list. We will then either enter the level number for the movie or the path to unload for the Location. To test a movie, we simply choose Control | Test Movie.

As more and more movie clips are loaded, it may become difficult to keep track of what has been loaded and more importantly at what level. To aid developers, Flash caters for this through the Movie Explorer and refers to the hierarchy of levels and movie clips as the display list. Figure 10.21 illustrates this for the Load Movie example shown in Figure 10.20.

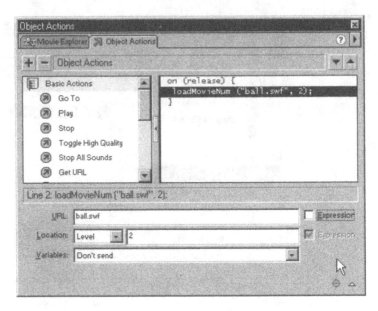

Figure 10.20 Example of loading a movie using the Load Movie action. The ball.swf (Flash movie) will be activated at level 2 on the release of the mouse button.

As mentioned earlier every movie has its own Timeline. So, how do we get two movies to communicate with each other? By allowing messages to pass between them. In other words, we send messages from one Timeline to another. The Timeline acting as a source for the messages is referred to as the controller. The Timeline that receives the messages is called the target. The messages are in the form of actions. As Figure 10.22 shows, there are two ways of assigning actions to a target through the Actions panel. The first uses actions under the Actions category, whilst the second makes use of the actions associated with the MovieClip object from the Objects category. If we wanted to perform multiple actions on the same target, we can use either the Tell Target command or the With command. The way this works is that we point to the target Timeline once and then apply the necessary actions.

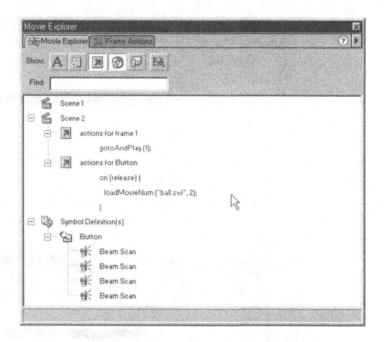

Figure 10.21 *The Movie Explorer showing the display list for the case illustrated in Figure 10.20. The ActionScript and sound effects used for the button can clearly be seen.*

We can control a movie belonging to another Timeline using the Action panel following the steps outlined below:

- Select an instance on the controller Timeline to which an action or actions will be attached.
- Open the Actions panel (Window | Actions) and select the Tell Target option within the Basic Actions category.
- We then invoke the Insert Target Path dialogue box by clicking the Insert Target button (positioned on the bottom right corner of the Actions panel). The resulting dialogue box is shown in Figure 10.23. This contains the current movie clip (labelled 'this') and any hierarchical movie clips that could be targeted. We use this to make entries to the Target text box in the Parameters pane.
- Notation refers to the syntax:; choose either Dots (as in JavaScript, which is the default) or Slashes (as is common with Flash 4) to express a target path.

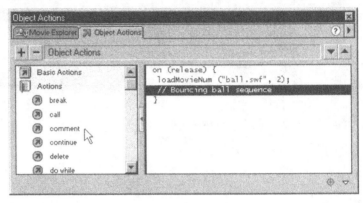

a)

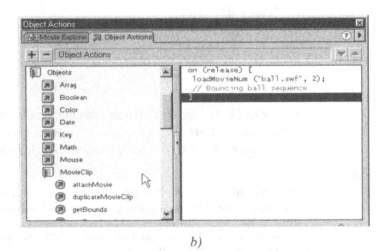

b)

Figure 10.22 *Assigning actions to a controller Timeline using the Actions panel: a) via Actions category, and b) through the Objects category.*

- Mode refers to the way the hierarchy for the movie clip will be displayed: Relative only shows movie clips that exist in the selected frame of the current Timeline, whilst Absolute displays every movie clip appearing in every frame of a movie. With absolute addressing, we start with either _root or _level and then go through the hierarchy to the desired movie clip. In the case of relative addressing, we can use _parent to refer to the parent

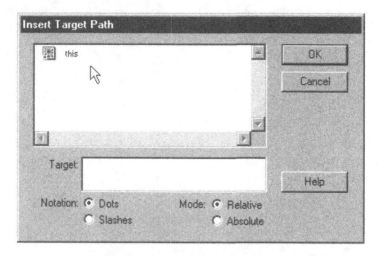

Figure 10.23 Insert Target Path dialogue box, contains the current movie clip (labelled 'this') and any hierarchical files which could be targeted.

Timeline of the current Timeline. We can make multiple use of this to move up a hierarchy to a desired level. The use of relative addressing aids portability and the reusability of action scripts.

- Having chosen the Notation and Mode, choose a movie clip from the Display. The Target text box displays the path to the target movie clip.
- Click OK to return to the Actions panel. More actions can be assigned to the controller for the target movie.

For a detailed explanation on the role of ActionScripts and their usage, together with a complete list of action commands, download a copy of Macromedia's ActionScript Reference Guide from their web-site at www.macromedia.com. An on-line reference and dictionary is also available via Help | ActionScript Reference and Help | ActionScript Dictionary.

Chapter 11

Publishing and Exporting Movies

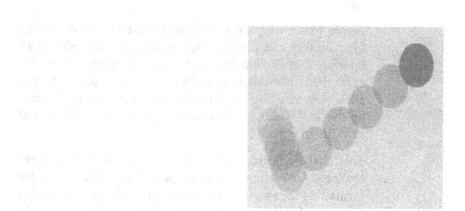

Introduction

Having created our Flash movie, using the many tools and features available, we are now ready to evaluate and publish it. This is no doubt the most rewarding aspect of the effort where we see how well the movie meets our initial goals and objectives, as well as making it available for an audience to review and possibly provide some feedback.

There are a variety of options which allow for automating and customizing the movie contents: Flash movie files (extension FLA) need to be converted to another format for playback. There are a number of formats that can be used, including HTML, BMP, GIF, JPEG, PNG, AVI or QuickTime. Through setting the publish and export parameters, we can output a complete movie as a Flash Player file, or as a series of bitmaps, or as a frame or image file, or as a still or moving image. So, whether we are creating a movie for the web or for CD broadcasting, Flash has tools and options that allow us to do this.

Before publishing, we may want to test the movie for its functionality and performance. Flash caters for this via an interface that also has options to assess the performance, for example, of downloads. In addition, we can set parameters to allow viewers using the Flash Player to print a set of frames or the entire movie. This may be useful for design and storyboard purposes.

This chapter begins with looking at the tools which are available for testing a movie, the various alternatives for formatting the movie for export and publishing are looked at next, and finally the available printing options which will allow the viewer to print desired frames of the movie.

Testing the movie for functionality and performance

Evaluation of animation sequences, movie clips, action scripts, etc., is undertaken through a separate interface from that used for creating and developing a scene. We use the Control | Test Scene or Control | Test Movie to switch to the testing environment. By doing so, we are in a position to test just about every aspect of the scene or movie. Figure 11.1 depicts the scenario where we note that additional tools become available and that most of the authoring tools are disabled.

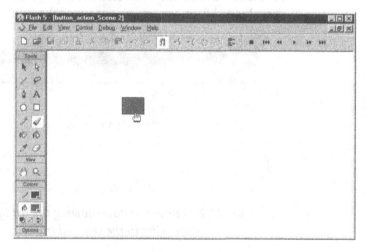

Figure 11.1 Flash testing environment, activated through Control | Test Scene *or* Control | Test Movie.

We can test the functionality of the scene or movie without too much difficulty. The behaviour of buttons, animation sequences, actions invoked by scripts, and the like, should be thoroughly checked. It is important that any bugs, no matter how small, should be corrected. If the scene or movie makes reference to URLs or requires working with a web server then we will need to publish our work on the web to evaluate its performance.

As Figure 11.2 shows, we can use Control | List Objects to open a corresponding Output window that displays all the objects of a frame, or group of frames. Likewise, choosing Control | List Variables will open a window which, in addition to displaying the variables, also shows their respective current values. The testing environment is similar to a traditional debugger used to test programs so that scripts used to control flow and for assigning actions can be traced and their respective working evaluated. Note that Flash provides a debugger within its authoring environment as well. To display it, we need to return to the editing mode and then choose Window | Debugger. If we wanted to debug a movie then we would choose Control | Debug Movie. More information on this can be found in Macromedia's reference document on ActionScript (which can be downloaded from www.macromedia.com).

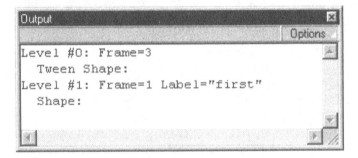

Figure 11.2 Output window showing the list of objects appearing in the selected frame.

An important tool for gauging download performance is the Bandwidth Profiler. This provides a graphical representation of the file sizes associated with each frame. The actual file sizes clearly are pivotal in determining the download performance of a movie. The larger the file size, the longer it will take to download, and vice versa. It is often amazing that even seemingly small objects (for example, a short sound clip) can occupy so much storage space. So, being able to view the size of frames before publishing is an asset. Moreover, we can test the performance of the movie based on a simulated modem speed. This way, we can identify problematic frames. The Bandwidth Profiler shows these through using a dividing red line on the graph.

As Figure 11.3 depicts, clicking on the Control menu yields three common options for the modem speed. In the simulation, the speeds listed in the brackets are used and not the ones specified for the modem. For example, choosing 56 kb/s in fact translates to 7 kbytes/s. The value used for the simulation is 4.7 kbytes/s. In doing this, Flash attempts to add realism by mirroring download speeds of the Internet more accurately. We can change these settings through using the dialogue box associated with Control | Customise.

We open the Bandwidth Profiler by choosing View | Bandwidth Profiler. As Figure 11.4 shows, there are two parts relaying information about the movie and its download performance. On the right side is the graphical representation which includes the Timeline header and the size of each of the frames. The size of a frame is shown as a single bar and is measured in kbytes. The red horizontal line reflects the current speed of data (modem) transfer. If a bar extends above this, it implies that the frame size is larger than the data transfer rate and the movie must pause for the frame to be loaded.

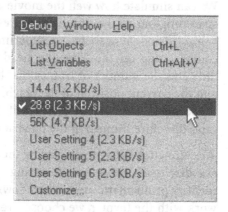

Figure 11.3 Control menu showing the various speeds available for the modem. The ones shown in the bracket are those actually used.

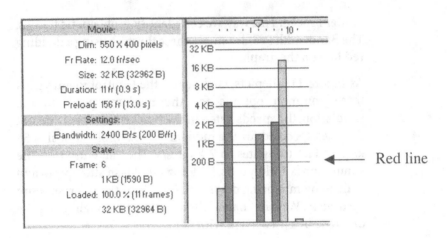

Red line

Figure 11.4 The Bandwidth Profiler.

On the right side of the Bandwidth Profiler is written information about the movie, its settings and its current state. This gives the movie's dimensions, the frame (playback) rate, size in kbytes, number of frames and duration in seconds, and the number of frames required as preload to commence playback from the time of download. In addition, the bandwidth for data transfer, the current frame and the number of frames loaded to date is also shown.

We can simulate how well the movie will play by adding the streaming bar to the graphical representation. By choosing View | Show Streaming, we superimpose a shaded (green) colour range on the Timeline header. The streaming bar indicates the number of frames that have been downloaded and the current position of the playhead. Figure 11.5 depicts the scenario. This way, we can identify any potential slowness (and therefore frames) in the playback.

We can switch between displaying the contents of each frame (as discussed above) or inserting a streaming graph to identify problematic areas when downloading the movie. To work with the former, we choose View | Frame by Frame Graph. This is what Figure 11.4 is showing: by clicking on a frame bar, we get details about the frame on the left side of the Bandwidth Profiler. If we choose View | Streaming

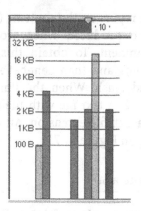

Figure 11.5 Streaming bar (shown shaded) indicating the number of frames that have been downloaded and the position of the playhead on the Timeline header.

Graph, we will obtain a better picture of how the movie will playback. As Figure 11.6 indicates, alternate shades of light and dark grey blocks are used to represent each frame. The width of each block reflects the time taken to download the respective frame. In some instances where file size is relatively small, more than one frame is downloaded within a time unit. In this case, the blocks are placed on top of each other. The important point here is that any blocks lying above the red horizontal line represent potential problems and will require attention with a view to reducing their respective file sizes, or increasing the modem speed.

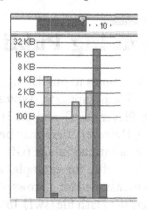

Figure 11.6 Bandwidth Profiler incorporating the Streaming Graph option.

A text report on the contents (in particular, the frame sizes) can be produced when working within the authoring environment. To obtain this, choose `File | Publish Settings` and then `Generate size report` from the tab headed Flash. When the Publish button is clicked, Flash generates a text file with the same name as the movie and with a `txt` file extension. An example of part of a report is shown in Figure 11.7.

```
Movie Report
------------

Frame #    Frame Bytes    Total Bytes    Page
-------    -----------    -----------    ----------------
      1            118            118    Scene 1
      2           5043           5161    Scene 2
      3              2           5163    2
      4              2           5165    3
      5              2           5167    4
      6           1590           6757    5
      7              2           6759    6
      8           2383           9142    7
      9          23803          32945    8
     10              2          32947    9
     11             15          32962    10

Page                           Shape Bytes    Text Bytes
--------------------------     -----------    ----------
Scene 1                                 76             0
Scene 2                                  0             0
```

Figure 11.7 Text report showing the actual sizes of each frame.

Understanding Publish Settings

When it comes to publishing, there are a number of formats which Flash supports. Typically, we are working with the Flash Player (swf) and an HTML page where the file will reside. However, there may be instances where we also need to have a bitmap image (GIF, JPEG or PNG) format as well. This is useful, for example, when there is no Flash Player plug-in installed for a browser and it is therefore not possible to view the Flash file (swf). In this case, the bitmap image will be displayed.

Before we publish the movie, we need to decide on the format of the delivery. To this regards, we choose `File | Publish Settings`. This opens up the corresponding window shown in Figure 11.8. We note that the HTML format is selected by default, since an HTML file is required to display the movie in a browser. If there are parameters for the (selected) formats which need to be specified then a corresponding tab (panel) appears within the window.

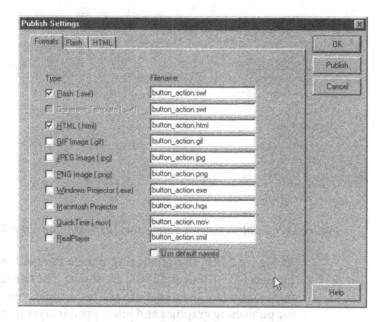

Figure 11.8 The Publish Settings window.

Figure 11.9 shows both the contents of the panels for Flash and HTML formats. Looking at the Flash parameters, we can adjust the quality of bitmaps, type of audio (sound) stream and the form of audio compression to employ. We can also add a password. This is used for debugging purposes so that an unauthorized viewer cannot debug a Flash movie. The HTML panel has a spectrum of options ranging from the size of the display window to its background colour. It also creates the attributes for the <object> and <embed> tags and allows for a template selection. The template is used to hold the settings made in this panel. Selection of a template is important as different templates have different functionalities. Basic templates simply place the movie in a browser, whilst more advanced templates could check whether a Flash Player plug-in has been installed. If not, it may then automatically download a version and install it for the browser.

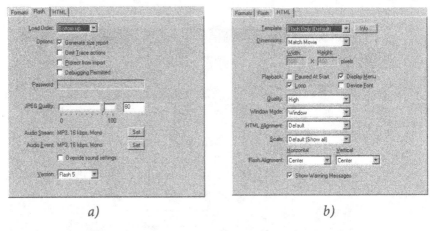

a)   *b)*

Figure 11.9 *Publish format panels for: (a) Flash and (b) HTML.*

In Figure 11.10, the publishing panels for the three image formats (GIF, JPEG, and PNG) are shown. The GIF format has been around for over a decade and is the most popular choice for publishing graphics and bitmapped images on the web. It has an added feature of being possible to animate, and as such is optimized by Flash through storing keyframes and in-between (which in turn only reflect changes in a sequence) frames. Options include interlacing and transparency. The former caters for the partial display of a static image which is being downloaded. As more data is transferred, the image becomes clearer and clearer. Transparency allows for the background to be opaque, or fully transparent, or partially transparent. The other point to note about GIF is that it has a maximum colour palette of 256. This means that, to view more than 256 colours, we will need to dither (mix) colours. This can increase the file size and probably, more importantly, may make the published image look worse on some low resolution displays. Care must be taken, therefore, when using dithering.

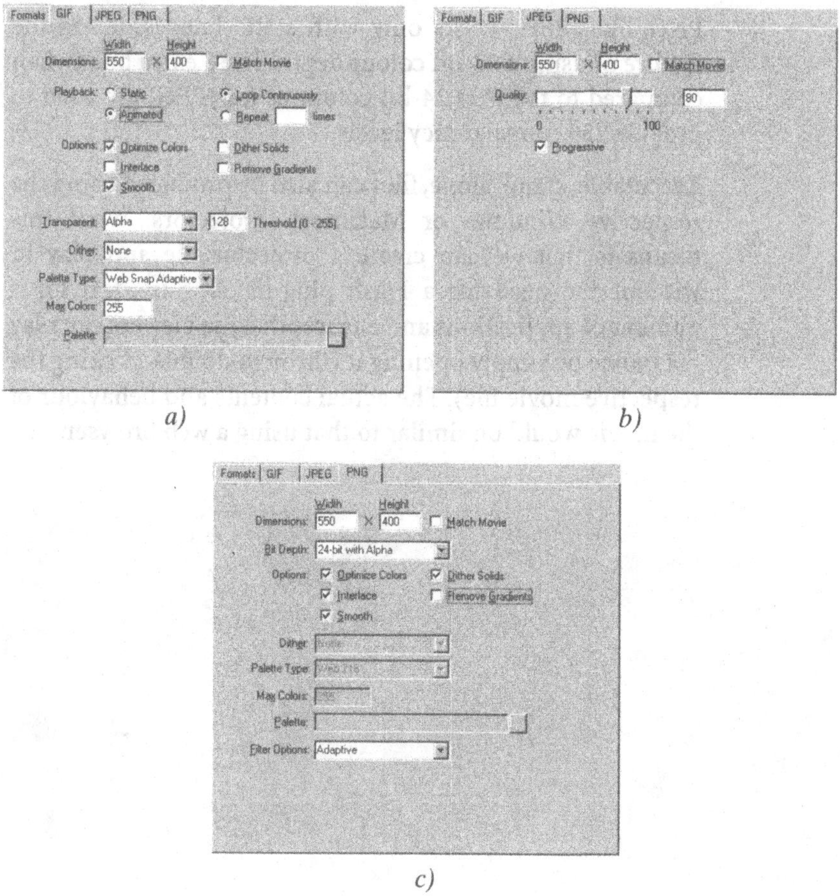

Figure 11.10 Publish format panels for: (a) GIF, (b) JPEG, and (c) PNG.

JPEG is ideal when working with photographic quality images. It works with what is referred to as true (24-bit) colours and uses a compression approach that allows for quality adjustments. By reducing the amount of compression (that is, the detail in an image that is made redundant), we increase the quality of the published image. This, however, will increase the resulting file size. So, an equilibrium between quality and compression needs to be found for images. The Progressive option will download the JPEG image in stages and the resulting image will gain more focus as more data is received.

PNG, like JPEG, works only with static images. It has the feature of using a 32-bit colour depth. The 8 extra bits (when compared to the true 24-bit colour as for JPEG) are used to provide 256 transparency levels.

Executable, stand-alone, files can also be produced using the respective Windows or Macintosh Projectors. What this means is that we can create a projector file and play it, without the need for a Flash plug-in. This is ideal for a number of applications and ensures that the viewers can play the movie by simply opening it (through double-clicking the respective movie file). The actual contents and behaviour of the movie would be similar to that using a web browser.

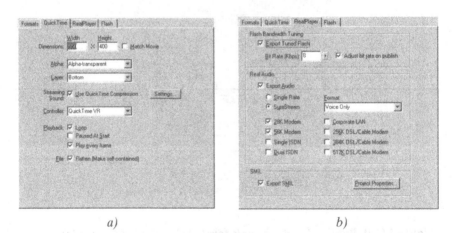

a)   *b)*

Figure 11.11 Publish format panel for (a) QuickTime 4, and (b) RealPlayer.

Figure 11.11 depicts the publishing panels for QuickTime 4 and RealPlayer. Both are well-known, accepted, formats. QuickTime 4 is used for working with video and multimedia types of data. A Flash movie is translated into a QuickTime track. Regardless of the size or the number of layers used, it is stored within a single QuickTime track. The contents and behaviour of the QuickTime version are as they would be if the movie were played using the Flash Player. In other words, all the features contained in the original Flash movie are maintained. The RealPlayer allows for the formatting and customizing of sound clips. Even a small audio clip, when digitized and used within a movie, can take up lots of storage space. So, care must be taken to optimize the overall file size in order to achieve realistic playbacks.

Previewing publish settings

Wouldn't it be convenient to preview the publish settings before we exported the movie? This way, we could view the effect of the parameters on the final movie before we put it on the web. Well, the Flash environment has just the command for this. Choose File | Publish Preview. This, as Figure 11.12 shows, opens up a sub-menu showing the available formats. We next choose the format to play our movie in and see how the parameter settings affect the published movie.

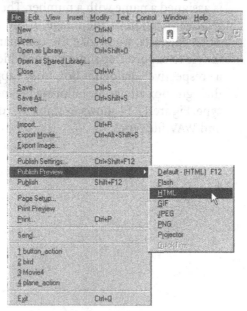

Figure 11.12 The Publish Preview menu and its associated sub-menu of formatting options.

In using the Publish Preview command, a number of temporary files are created and placed in the same folder as the Flash movie file. These are not removed automatically after the execution of the command. Thus, we will need to manually remove them.

Exporting movies

If we had a need to transfer the contents of the movie to another application then, instead of publishing it, we would choose to export it. This way, we could relay the contents of the Flash movie to the other application for viewing and editing purposes. There are two commands that allow us to export: we can either choose File | Export Movie or File | Export Image. The former works with movies similar to the publish command in that conversion to a desired format can take place. In addition, we could export a movie as consisting of a series of still images. In this case, each image is assigned a name with a number. The number indicates the relative position of the image to the first image. As Figure 11.13 suggests, we invoke the command and then choose a movie to export. Depending upon which file type we choose, a respective dialogue box may appear. The respective dialogue box allows for tailoring the movie for the export file type. Figure 11.14 shows examples of dialogue boxes for AVI and WAV file types.

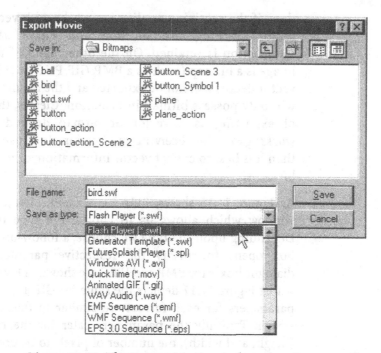

Figure 11.13 *The Export Movie window, showing some of the file types that could be used for exporting a Flash movie.*

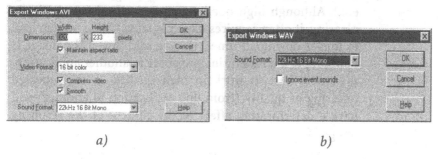

a)   *b)*

Figure 11.14 *Dialogue boxes which can be used to customize the exporting of movies in the following file types: (a) AVI, and (b) WAV.*

Using the File | Export Image command allows for the contents of a current frame, or a selected image, to be exported as a file (instead of a series of images as with exporting movies). If the Flash image is stored as a vector then, if the receiving application works with vectors, the vector (making use of line and curve segments) information is retained. On the other hand, if the Flash image is a bitmap (such as a BMP, GIF, PNG or JPEG) then vector details will not be exported and the resulting image will only possess bitmap information. Clearly, the choice of exporting as a vector or bitmap depends on the workings of the receiving application. If it uses vectors then it is best to export vector information; otherwise use bitmaps.

As Figure 11.15 shows, File | Export Image opens a window which allows us to choose the type of image. Depending upon the type we choose, a follow-up dialogue box opens to specify the respective parameters. The dialogue boxes for BMP and JPEG are shown in Figure 11.16, whilst Figure 11.17 depicts the same for GIF and PNG. The parameters for each format are similar to that discussed earlier. Typically the parameters cater for the resolution (height and width), the number of pixels to be used for the colour depth, the quality of output required (that is, the smooth, balance between amount of compression and image content), and how the image should be downloaded and displayed (for example, interlaced, progressive decoding, etc.). Although high quality output is always aesthetically pleasing, it often requires large file sizes. These in turn lead to longer download times. Having said this, if the image is being exported for editing purposes to another application, then it is best to work in high quality, as the repeated lowering of quality (from one application to another) will have a deteriorating effect of the content of the resulting image.

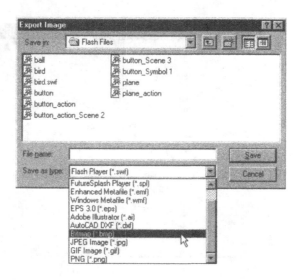

Figure 11.15 *The Export Image window, showing some of the file types that can be used.*

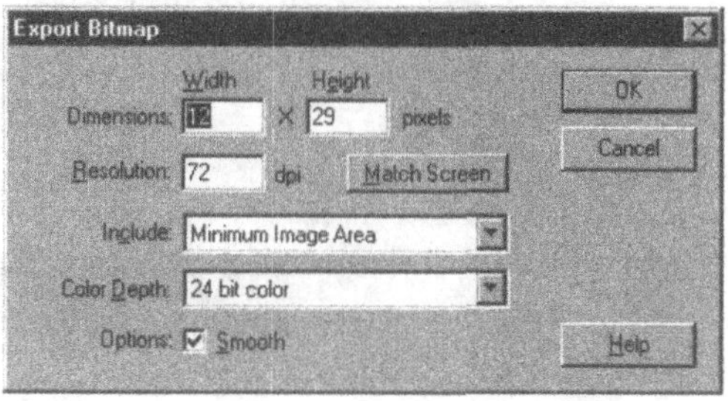

a)

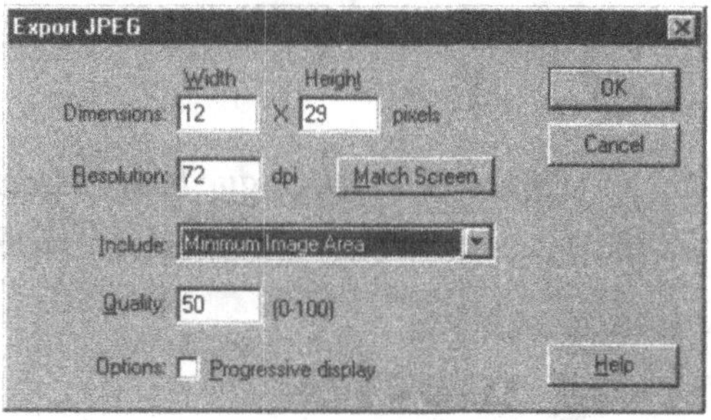

b)

Figure 11.16 *Dialogue boxes for exporting images: (a) BMP, and (b) JPEG.*

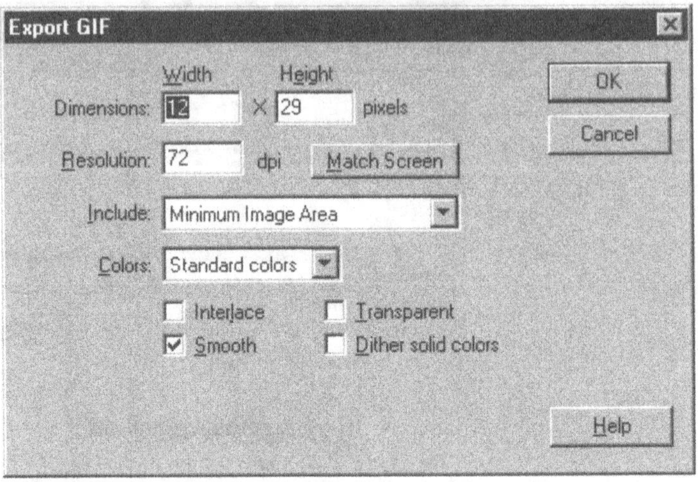

a)

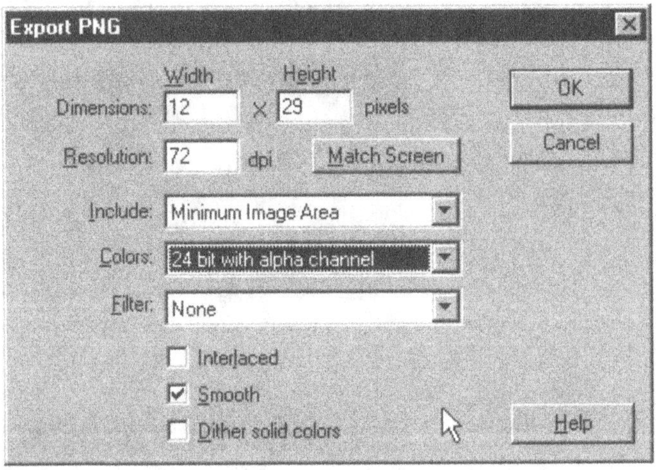

b)

Figure 11.17 Dialogue boxes associated with the Export Image window: (a) GIF, and (b) PNG.

Printing movies

Having interactive movies is not just attractive, but a necessity to meet the growing requirements of businesses to market and sell products across the globe. As a part of this, it may be also be necessary for the users to print a section of a movie. This could allow the users to obtain a hard-copy of a manuscript, or an invoice, or some coupons. The concept is somewhat different from printing pages through a browser. With Flash, we can specify the frames to be printed so that we can protect against unauthorized printing. In addition, printable areas within frames can also be stipulated, as well the form of the print-out: bitmap or vector. Furthermore, we can assign actions to activate the printing process.

To set a frame or a series of frames as printable, we select the desired frames and then open the Frame panel (either through Window | Panels and then Frame or Modify | Frame). On the panel is a text box titled Label. Within this, enter #p to specify the frame as printable. This is shown in Figure 11.18.

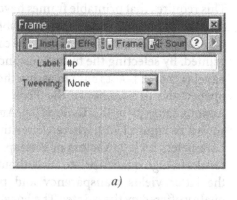

a)

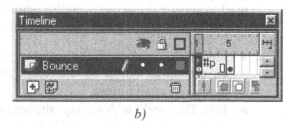

b)

Figure 11.18 Defining a frame as printable: (a) through entering #p in the Label section of the Frame panel, and (b) the verification of the same through the #p label being assigned to the selected (first) frame.

Printing selected frames is useful, for example, if for a given animation we only wanted the keyframes to be printed and not the in-between frames. We can refine the printing in that specific areas of frames are printed and not the complete frames. To achieve this, we follow the steps outlined below:

- Select and label a frame as printable using #p in the Label section of the Frame panel (as described above).
- Create a shape on the Stage which will be used as a bounding box to define the printable area.
- Select the frame in the Timeline containing the bounding box.
- Open the Frame panel, and enter #b in the label section.

We can also make use of the Print command to assign actions, for example, to a button so that it can be used to print frames belonging to the same movie or to another movie. This requires that printable frames have been specified using the #p parameter and any printable areas by the #b parameter. By default, if this is not the case then all frames are printed. By selecting the button instance, we use the Actions panel (Window | Actions) to assign the print action. Having opened the panel, choose the Print command within the Actions category of the Toolbox list. An illustration of this is shown in Figure 11.19, where we see that the corresponding parameters include Vectors or Bitmap. Choosing the former results in high quality printouts without transparency, whilst the latter yields transparency and printouts at the best quality offered by the printer. The Location parameter can be used to specify the active Timeline whose frames would be printed. The Bounding Box parameter offers three options:

- Movie. This works with the bounding box area defined by #b though an object on the Stage. The area would be applicable to all frames.
- Max. This works with a composite bounding box to define the print area, for all printable frames. It is useful if the printable frames have different sizes.
- Frame. This works with using a bounding box for each printable frame as the print area for the frame. In other words, it changes the print area for each frame and resizes

the objects to fit the print area. Useful if different sized objects reside on each frame and we want, for example, each object to print fully on a page.

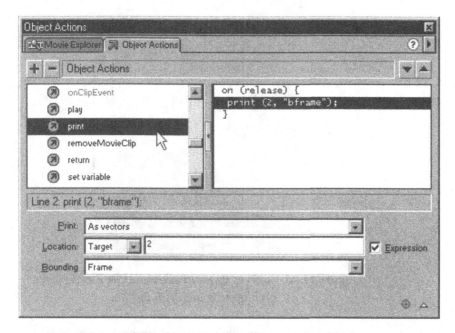

Figure 11.19 *Action panel showing the Print command and its associated parameters.*

Frames can be printed using the steps outlined below:

- Use the #p and #b parameters to specify the frames and bounding box respectively for the movie.
- Choose File | Publish Preview and then Default to view the movie in a browser.
- Right-click to open up the Flash Player context menu. Figure 11.20 depicts this scenario. From this, select the print option to display the respective dialogue box.
- As Figure 11.21 shows, the resulting dialogue box has the following three options for the print range:
  - All – prints every frame in the movie if none are labelled.
  - Pages – prints labelled frames within the specified range.
  - Selection – prints current frame.
- Choose any other options and then click OK.

Depending on the option selected and the type of printing (whether full frames or only specified areas) required, we will get a corresponding output from the printer.

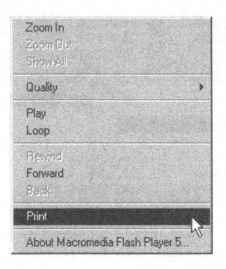

Figure 11.20 *Context menu available in the Flash Player, highlighting the Print option.*

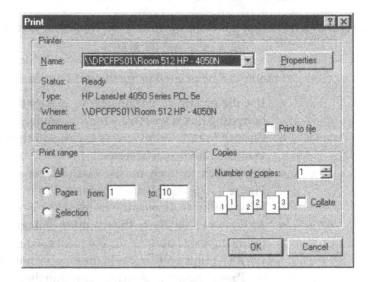

Figure 11.21 *The Print dialogue box associated with the Flash Player.*

Conversely, if we did not want to print any frames of a movie, then we would enter !#p as the label for a frame in the Timeline. This would have the effect of making the entire movie unprintable and thus the Print option in the Flash Player becomes inactive. Moreover, we can remove the context menu altogether by choosing File | Publish and then under the HTML tab, uncheck Display Menu. Figure 11.22 gives an illustration of this. Note that users can still print parts of a movie (that is, web pages) using the Print command available in a particular browser.

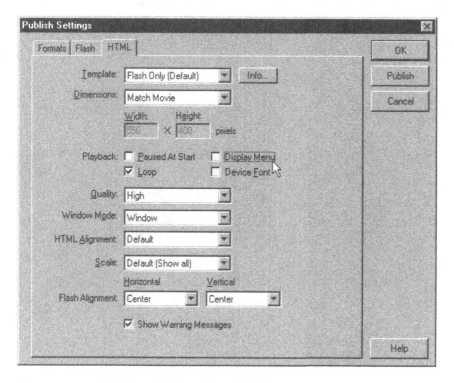

Figure 11.22 *Disabling the context menu belonging to the Flash Player by unchecking the Display Menu option within the HTML panel under Publish Settings.*

Index

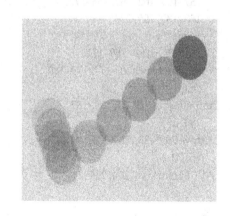

The Essential Series

Editor: John Cowell

If you are looking for an accessible and quick introduction to a new language or area then these are the books for you.

Covering a wide range of topics including virtual reality, computer animation, Java, and Visual Basic to name but a few, the books provide a quick and accessible introduction to the subject. **Essential** books let you start developing your own applications with the minimum of fuss - and fast.

The last few pages of this book are devoted to giving brief information about three of the other titles in this series.

All books are, of course, available from all good booksellers (who can order them even if they are not in stock), but if you have difficulties you can contact the publishers direct, by telephoning +44 1483 418822 (in the UK and Europe), +1/212/4 60 15 00 (in the USA), or by emailing orders@svl.co.uk

www.springer.de   www.springer-ny.com
www.essential-series.com

Essential
Linux *fast*

Ian Chivers

Linux has become increasingly popular as an alternative operating system to Microsoft Windows as its ease of installation and use has improved. This, combined with an ever growing range of applications, makes it an attractive alternative to Windows for many people.

Ian Chivers focuses on...
- The essential preliminaries that should be carried out before installing Linux
- Installing a Linux system
- Configuring peripherals
- Using X Windows
- Basic and intermediate Unix commands
- Using the Internet with Linux
- Using Linux for document preparation
- Using Linux for programming

If you are thinking of switching from Windows, this book tells you how to get and install Linux and explains why Linux is becoming the hottest operating system of the Millennium.

240 pages
Softcover
ISBN 1-85233-408-8

Please see page 237 for ordering details

Essential UML *fast*
Using Select Case Tool for Rapid Applications Development

Aladdin Ayesh

Essential UML *fast* introduces the reader to the concepts of object-oriented analysis, design and programming, using the Unified Modeling Language. UML is one of the best known modeling languages in the object-oriented software development world, and is fast becoming a standard modeling language for OO software developers.

This book contains plenty of examples and detailed illustrations, making it easy for you to work through the techniques step-by-step, and get up and running with UML fast.

Once you have read this book you'll know all about...
- Use case tools and software modeling basics
- Setting up and running Select Enterprise
- Use case diagrams
- Class diagrams
- Object interaction diagrams
- Behavioural modeling
- Patterns and techniques for fast software modeling and development

Source code for the examples in this book are available at the Essential series site: http:\\www.essential-series.com

240 pages
Softcover
ISBN 1-85233-413-4

Please see page 237 for ordering details